Just a Journalist

The William E. Massey Sr. Lectures
in American Studies, 2015

Just a Journalist

On the Press, Life, and the Spaces Between

Linda Greenhouse

Harvard University Press

Cambridge, Massachusetts
London, England
2017

First printing

Chapter 3 quotes in full the author's previously published article: "November 22: Two Years Later," *The Harvard Crimson* (November 22, 1965). The William E. Massey, Sr. Lectures in American Studies. © 2016 The Harvard Crimson, Inc. All rights reserved. Reprinted with permission.

Library of Congress Cataloging-in-Publication Data

Names: Greenhouse, Linda, author.
Title: Just a journalist : on the press, life, and the spaces between / Linda Greenhouse.
Other titles: William E. Massey Sr. lectures in American studies ; 2015.
Description: Cambridge, Massachusetts : Harvard University Press, 2017. | Series: The William E. Massey Sr. lectures in American studies ; 2015 | Includes bibliographical references and index.
Identifiers: LCCN 2017013621 | ISBN 9780674980334 (alk. paper)
Subjects: LCSH: Journalistic ethics—United States—21st century. | Reporters and reporting—United States—21st century. | Greenhouse, Linda.
Classification: LCC PN4756 .G725 2017 | DDC 174 / .907—dc23
LC record available at https://lccn.loc.gov/2017013621

For Caroline Rand Herron (1941–2016)

colleague, debating partner, and dear friend

CONTENTS

If the country is to be governed with the consent of the governed, then the governed must arrive at opinions about what their governors want them to consent to. How do they do this?

They do it by hearing on the radio and reading in the newspapers what the corps of correspondents tell them is going on in Washington and in the country at large and in the world. Here we perform an essential service. In some field of interest we make it our business to find out what is going on under the surface and beyond the horizon, to infer, to deduce, to imagine and to guess, what is going on inside, and what this meant yesterday, and what it could mean tomorrow.

In this we do what every sovereign citizen is supposed to do, but has not the time or the interest to do for himself. This is our job. It is no mean calling, and we have a right to be proud of it, and to be glad that it is our work.

—*Walter Lippmann,*
seventieth-birthday address to the National Press Club,
September 23, 1959

PREFACE

This book began as the William E. Massey Sr. Lectures in American Studies, delivered on three afternoons in November 2015 under the auspices of Harvard University's Program in American Studies.

When I received the invitation to give the Massey Lectures, my initial impulse was to offer an analysis of the United States Supreme Court, which I covered as a journalist for the *New York Times* for nearly thirty years. But on reflection, this seemed an occasion to say something more personal—to offer a perspective on the current practice of journalism in the United States and on the forces that influence and, to a distressing extent, distort it.

When I embarked on this project in the summer of 2015, the 2016 presidential campaign was in view but barely under way. By the time I gave the lectures, the election was still nearly a year off and Donald J. Trump was such an implausible candidate that I took no account of how mainstream journalism was treating him. I could not have imagined what was to come: how the media's treatment of Donald Trump reflected and, I believe, eventually not only validated the themes in the lectures but also offered the prospect of profound change in political journalism. I could not have foreseen that the *New York Times,* having so faithfully adhered for so many years to the journalistic norm of "fair and balanced" objectivity, would have felt not only free but in fact driven to label a major party's presidential candidate a liar.

As one who has long sought to understand the implications of the objectivity norm, who has challenged it in writing and been seen to transgress it in my personal behavior, I was fascinated and thrilled by the trajectory of the 2016 campaign coverage and by the media's willingness to confront a hostile president. But I have no certainty that anything fundamental has changed. Rather, I have questions, which I raise here but which can't be answered in a book being completed so close to the events it describes. I am a nearly fifty-year practitioner of journalism, but not a journalism scholar. I draw on journalism scholarship in this book, and I await the scholarship that will surely come. I hope my observations may point in some fruitful directions.

In this book, I explore the relationship between journalist and citizen and question whether

prevailing norms fix too rigid a boundary between the two roles. The story I tell here is a personal one. Much of the narrative concerns the
New York Times, where I spent the great majority
of my professional life. I admire and respect the
Times deeply, and cherish the forty years I spent
there. To the extent that my commentary is critical, I hope the criticism can be seen as coming
from one who regards the *Times* as an essential
element of our civic fabric and who wants only
the best for it—and from it.

Just a Journalist

1

Boundaries

An Accidental Activist

In the spring of 2008, a criminal justice reform organization in New York City called the Justice Project held a dinner to honor New York's former governor Hugh L. Carey. It was a fundraiser, with tickets priced at several hundred dollars. I sent my check immediately.

Thirty-four years earlier, as a very young political reporter on the metropolitan staff of the *New York Times,* I had covered Carey's long-shot gubernatorial campaign. A Democrat from Brooklyn, he had served seven rather unremarkable terms in Congress. He was an Irish Catholic widower with eleven children, lacking charisma and verbal finesse but smart and wickedly funny. Covering a statewide political campaign was, for me, a dream assignment; a desire to write about politics and politicians was what had drawn me to journalism.

The assignment was hardly a testament to my editors' opinion of my talent or potential. Far from it. The smart money said Carey had no chance of capturing the Democratic nomination, let alone defeating the incumbent Republican governor, Malcolm Wilson. But still, a warm body was needed on the campaign trail, so they sent me.

It turned out that New York in 1974 was ready for a change after sixteen years of Republican control, the first fifteen under Nelson A. Rockefeller—"Rocky"—who had dominated and ultimately exhausted the state with his grand designs and his noblesse oblige, and the sixteenth year, after Rockefeller became vice president, under Wilson, his loyal, highly intelligent, but colorless lieutenant governor.

Hugh Carey was hardly a change agent, but at that moment he looked like change. When the New York City financial crisis hit just weeks into his first term, he rose to the occasion. Proclaiming that "the days of wine and roses are over," he summoned the best financial minds in the country, jawboned the unions, worked across party lines, and earned the title that would later be bestowed by an admiring biographer: "The Man Who Saved New York."[1]

I covered the New York fiscal crisis and Carey's first three years in office. Along the way, I turned thirty. These were the foundational years of my life in journalism, and in many ways the most thrilling. I was the first woman the *Times* had assigned to Albany, 150 miles north of Times Square and functionally on another planet. It was a place where the all-male press corps enlivened the dull winters by dressing in drag and putting on a show for the amusement of the politicians. (When I was invited to join the cast to play an actual woman, I observed that this was an invitation I could hardly accept, since women had long been prohibited from attending the show. The exclusionary policy was promptly dropped— evidently, no one had questioned it before, and it was simply taken for granted as just the way things were in Albany—but I politely declined to join the boys on stage.) I was a half-generation younger than the seasoned political reporters who were my colleagues in the four-person *Times* Albany bureau. They became my mentors, my teachers, my buddies. It was the graduate journalism education I never had, and the best I could have imagined.

After Carey left office in 1983, he pretty much disappeared from view. I had moved to the *Times* Washington bureau by then, and our paths didn't cross. In the spring of 2008, he was eighty-nine years old, and I heard that his health was poor. Of course I had to go to New York.

At the dinner, I found Carey seated in a wheelchair, physically frail but with his mind and sense of humor as sharp as ever. Sitting together in a corner of the reception room during the cocktail hour, we reminisced about the early days of his campaign, days when he and I occupied the only two passenger seats in the only plane he could afford to charter as he barnstormed around the state that summer. I was now sixty-one years old, but he teased me, as he had back then, about my youth and inexperience.

When the proceedings began, I was asked to speak. I was surprised, and of course had prepared nothing. In the few minutes I had to get ready while others were speaking, I considered my options. I could entertain the audience, which included many veterans of Carey's administration, with anecdotes from the plentiful store we all shared. I was still a *New York Times* reporter, and that would be the safe and expected thing to do. But I wasn't there as a reporter. I had paid my own way to attend the dinner as a citizen. So it was as a citizen that I spoke. Hugh Carey, I said, was the finest public servant I had ever known.

As I said those words, I felt a rush of adrenaline that left me a little light-headed. It wasn't from any uncharacteristic anxiety about public speaking. It was from the sense, and the thrill, of having crossed a line. *A reporter shouldn't say that,* even of a long-retired politician, even at what was likely to be—and was, as far as I know (Carey died in 2011 at ninety-two)—the final ingathering of those who had lived and worked with the man. An appraisal of the sort I offered was off-limits, I had no doubt. There would have been no issue had I been a historian, a biographer, an economist, a political scientist, a public official myself, or someone who had wandered in from off the street. But I was none of those things. I was just a journalist, a journalist with the nerve to say publicly that some politicians are better than other politicians, and that this aged long-ago governor of New York had been the best of all.

I wouldn't blame anyone for taking my description of having stepped into some sort of ethical abyss as hyperbole or neurotic self-absorption, but it is neither. I had learned as much some eighteen months earlier when I found myself the target of nearly the entire journalistic establishment for a speech I had given to my fellow alumnae of Harvard University's Radcliffe College. Unlike the night of the Carey dinner, I had not deliberately or knowingly broken any rules on the occasion of the Radcliffe speech. When the collective judgment that I had done so coalesced months later, I was truly surprised. If I was an "activist," as media pundits were quick to label me in the ensuing controversy, I was an accidental activist at best—and not a particularly adroit one at that.[2]

The Radcliffe speech, along with its personal consequences, illuminates a subject at the center of this project—and, to a degree that I could not have anticipated in late 2015 when I gave the lectures that became this book, a subject with political resonance as well. That subject is the journalist as public and private citizen: on the one hand, an employee with professional obligations that both empower and bind, and on the other, a member of a society that assumes the legitimacy, even the necessity, of an individual voice and of actions freely undertaken in the public square.

In training an autobiographical lens on the practice of journalism, my goal is to explore the ambiguous and shifting boundary that separates the one role from the other in the increasingly fragile but still vitally important world of mainstream journalism. When do professional norms, having evolved to buttress the credibility of a craft that only in modern times has laid claim to the status of a profession, unduly constrain not only journalism's practitioners but journalism itself? Does "objectivity," with its mantra of "fairness and balance," too often inhibit journalists from separating fact from fiction and from fulfilling the duty to help maintain an informed citizenry in a democracy?

Scholars were considering and debating these questions well before the 2016 presidential campaign. These academic debates often proceeded at a level of abstraction that in retrospect appears quaint; after all, the voting public had ample access to facts yet chose by the millions to disregard them. Again, I'm not a scholar of journalism; in fact I never took a journalism course. Years away from daily journalism's front lines myself, I watched with fascination as editors and reporters struggled with how to respond to Donald J. Trump's exaggerations and outright lies. It was with relief that I saw loyalty to the old rules erode and eventually buckle as editors and writers met their higher obligation to tell their audience the truth as they understood it. "Trump Gives Up a Lie but Refuses to Repent," read the extraordinary headline of a page-one *New York Times* story on September 17, 2016, reporting the Republican presidential nominee's grudging concession that President Barack Obama was in fact born in the United States.[3] But was this really "the death of 'he said, she said' journalism," as Peter Beinart declared two days later in the *Atlantic?*[4] As Zhou Enlai is said to have observed when asked about the impact of the French Revolution, it's too soon to tell. The best I can do, nearly half a century after I first stepped into a professional newsroom, is to tell my own story.

The occasion for the controversial speech was my receipt of the Radcliffe Medal, the former Radcliffe College's highest award.[5] This annual award—Justice Ruth Bader Ginsburg, Gloria Steinem, and Margaret Marshall, retired chief justice of Massachusetts, are among recent recipients—is bestowed under a big tent set up in Radcliffe Yard, before an invited audience of several hundred alumnae and friends. It was clear to me that this occasion, and this audience, deserved not a platitudinous thank-you but rather a serious reflection on a serious subject. The subject that occurred to me was the trajectory of my generation, the idealistic children of the 1960s who left Harvard and Radcliffe carrying with them both the desire to make the world a better place and the assumption that this goal was readily attainable. What had happened? That was my question, and my effort to address it was my text.

To set the scene: It was June 2006. George W. Bush—an age-mate, by the way, from the class of 1968 at Yale, as I was at Radcliffe—was midway through his second term. Two years earlier, in the case of *Rasul v. Bush,* the Supreme Court had rejected his administration's argument that the prison at Guantánamo Bay, then holding hundreds of men deemed enemy combatants, was immune from judicial oversight.[6] The court held instead that federal judges had jurisdiction to rule on the detainees' requests for relief through petitions for habeas corpus. On the domestic front, the president had turned over the social-issues agenda to the Right. Justice Sandra Day O'Connor, who had retired in January, had been instrumental fourteen years earlier in the five-to-four vote that preserved the constitutional right to abortion.[7] President Bush had replaced her with Samuel Alito, a movement conservative who, it was perfectly obvious, would vote to overturn *Roe v. Wade* in a heartbeat if the opportunity arose; he had been selected with that very prospect in view.

None of these observations would have come as news to a reader of the *New York Times* or a listener to NPR. These were the developments that were on my mind as I worked on my Radcliffe speech. I decided to set up the speech with a personal anecdote. A few years earlier, my husband and I had attended a concert by Paul Simon and Art Garfunkel, a reunion of two aging pop music giants whose haunting harmonies had provided—along with Motown, the Beatles, and Bob Dylan—the soundtrack of my college and early postcollege years, a soundtrack that plays in my mind to this day. Attending the concert, sitting in a big indoor sports arena filled with people my age whose long-ago young adulthood had unfurled to the same sounds, had been a powerfully, almost overwhelmingly, emotional experience. I described the occasion to the audience under the Radcliffe tent that June afternoon, in a speech I called "A Bridge over Troubled Water."

"It was a Sunday night," I began, "and the Metro train my husband and I took in from the suburbs to the big downtown sports arena was filled with people just like us, aging Baby Boomers taking mass transit in from the suburbs to be transported back across the years to the opening chords of 'Hello darkness, my old friend.'

"We were sitting high up in the arena, and I had a good view of thousands and thousands of people who were, as I said, just like me. Simon and Garfunkel had long been estranged and had not appeared together for many years, so the nostalgia was particularly deep. About halfway through, they sang their wonderful song 'America,' the one about the two kids riding through the night on a Greyhound bus, 'counting the cars on the New Jersey Turnpike.' When they came to the chorus, 'They've all come to look for America,' I began to cry.

"I'm not a person who bursts into tears at the drop of a hat, and I was truly surprised. I cried throughout the entire second half of the concert. I couldn't stop. It was a puzzling and disconcerting experience, and I worked hard in the ensuing days to figure it out. Finally, it came to me. Thinking back to my college days in those troubled and tumultuous late 1960s, there were many things that divided my generation. For the men in particular, of course, it was what stance to take toward the draft—acquiescence, artful avoidance, or active resistance. For many of us, it was how actively we should commit ourselves to the great causes of civil rights and the antiwar movement. (The women's movement was barely on the horizon for me at that point.) . . .

"Yet despite all these controversies, we were absolutely united in one conviction: the belief that in future decades, if the world lasted that long, when our turn came to run the country, we wouldn't make the same mistakes. Our generation would do a better job. I cried that night in the Simon and Garfunkel concert out of the realization that my faith had been misplaced. Our generation had not proved to be the solution. We were the problem.

"And of course my little crying jag occurred before we knew the worst of it, before it was clear the extent to which our government had turned its energy and attention away from upholding the rule of law and toward creating law-free zones at Guantánamo Bay, Abu Ghraib,

Haditha, and other places around the world. And let's not forget the sustained assault on women's reproductive freedom and the hijacking of public policy by religious fundamentalism. To say that these last years have been dispiriting is an understatement. I hope that today's undergraduates are taking the same vow that we did then, and I hope for all our sakes that they get closer to fulfilling it than we did."

I went on to talk about how the world in some important ways had actually gotten better, through progress for women in the workplace and through the Supreme Court's recognition of the rights of gay men and lesbians to "dignity" and "respect" in the 2003 *Lawrence v. Texas* decision.[8] There was a greater sense of inclusion of the formerly excluded. And I ended by quoting from another Simon and Garfunkel song, "Bridge over Troubled Water," that was the opposite of depressing. "All your dreams are on their way," they sang. "See how they shine. If you need a friend / I'm sailing right behind." And I thanked the assembled company of alumnae and friends for the medal.

So there it is. That was my speech. A little mawkish, actually. Edgy? I didn't think so. Over the line? I was about to find out.

It took a while. The speech was in early June. The mountains didn't tremble. In fact, nothing happened. June passed, then July, August, and most of September. Then I received a call from a man identifying himself as the NPR media reporter. His mother had gone to Radcliffe, he told me, and had seen the video of my speech on the Radcliffe website. He had a few questions for me. I forget his exact words, but the gist was to ask me to explain to him how, as a working journalist, I could have publicly criticized the Bush administration. I saw where this was going. His invocation of a supposed bond between his mother and me—a good reporter's technique—was a ploy that annoyed me. "I don't have to explain myself to you," I remember telling him, and I added, "You've evidently seen the video. I said what I said in a public place. Let the chips fall where they may."

This was not an auspicious beginning. In fact, my aggressive response was downright foolish. In retrospect, it would have been smarter to have fallen on my sword and begged for mercy, a reaction that didn't occur to me because I didn't think I had anything to apologize for, certainly not to him. At least, I shouldn't have described as a "public place" the invitation-only event at which I had spoken. Our conversation, such as it was, ended abruptly, and it was clear that the next chapter was likely to be unpleasant.

Sure enough, a week or so later, the NPR website posted a story under the headline, "Critics Question Reporter's Airing of Personal Views."[9] Who were these critics? They were leaders of the journalism establishment, having been presented by the NPR reporter with the offending paragraph. Jack Nelson, former Washington bureau chief of the *Los Angeles Times,* was described as having "blanche[d]" at "hearing of Greenhouse's remarks." (Evidently, the full speech was neither proffered nor requested. Nelson was honest enough to acknowledge to me, when I asked him, that he had not actually read it. Tom Kunkel, dean of the journalism school at the University of Maryland, also told me he hadn't read the speech before telling Howard Kurtz, then the media critic for the *Washington Post,* that my remarks had been "ill-advised.") Sandy Rowe, editor of the Portland *Oregonian* and former chair of the Pulitzer Prize board executive committee, evidently in answer to a question as to whether she found anything "problematic" about the speech, was quoted as saying, "If she or any other reporter stakes out a strong position on an issue that is still evolving both in society and before the courts, yes, I think that is problematic." NPR went on to report that "Rowe says the reputation of Greenhouse's newspaper is at stake when the reporter expresses her strong beliefs publicly."

The reputation of the *Times* was at stake because two years after the Supreme Court held that the Bush administration couldn't maintain a law-free zone at Guantánamo, the paper's Supreme Court correspondent criticized the administration for having tried to maintain a law-free zone? Strong stuff. It got stronger.

In the wake of the Jayson Blair scandal, in which an inadequately supervised young reporter fabricated a number of stories and seriously embarrassed the *New York Times,* the paper had established the position of "public editor." The purpose was to bring a seasoned non–*New York Times* journalist onto the scene, with editorial independence and the power to hold the paper to account for future lapses. The first public editor was Daniel Okrent, a longtime book and magazine editor, a free thinker who once came up with a great line: "The pursuit of balance can create imbalance because sometimes something is true."

Okrent's eighteen months as public editor were over by the time of my speech. He was described in the NPR story as having been "amazed" to learn of it. He later explained in an interview with *Newsweek* that he hadn't meant "amazed" in the sense of shocked or appalled; rather, he was "kind of amazed and thrilled." The *Newsweek* interview was entitled "Fair and Balanced? A Former *New York Times* Ombudsman Says Linda Greenhouse's Political Comments Aren't Necessarily a Bad Thing."[10] Okrent explained further:

My point was that when I was at the *Times* for 18 months, Linda was writing about the most sensitive, divisive issues in America—those that have come before the Supreme Court. She wrote about them analytically, not quoting other experts, but stating her own analyses of why things were this way and that way and what the court meant by that—and I never received a single complaint. Which is to say that no one ever perceived any ideological bias in her work. . . . There's a distinction between what a journalist may think about the issues of the day and how the journalist writes about the issues of the day. And that's the way it ought to be. Her views should not come into her work, which they don't, even though we now know that she has very strong political views. . . . It seems to me that what she does in her private life is her private life.[11]

Okrent added, "Maybe this opens up the conversation." It did, but in a way that turned out to be one-sided in the opposite direction. Byron Calame, a former editor at the *Wall Street Journal,* had recently become the *New York Times* public editor. The headline on his column in the Sunday *Times* of October 8, 2006, was "Hazarding Personal Opinions in Public Can Be Hazardous for Journalists." He had phoned me in the wake of the NPR report. I had never met the man. (I had met Okrent once or twice.) Our exchange was testy, to say the least. He didn't buy my explanation that my characterizations of the Bush administration's actions—the law-free zones, the right-wing-driven social policy agenda—were factual and would have been familiar territory to any *New York Times* reader. Nor was he interested in viewing the speech in the context of its narrative structure or of the particular relationship between speaker and audience. And he voiced his explicit disagreement with his predecessor's benign view of the matter. "As the influential Supreme Court reporter for *The Times,* a beat that touches nearly all areas of public policy," he wrote, "Ms. Greenhouse has an over-riding obligation to avoid publicly expressing these kinds of personal opinions. During the current term, allowing her to cover court devel-opments that involve the topics on which she voiced opinions in June risks giving the paper's critics fresh opportunities to snipe at its public policy coverage." In other words, there were schoolyard bullies abroad in the land, and this was no time to stand up to them. Might such a time ever come? He didn't say. He did do me the favor of quoting my reaction to his suggestion that I now be restricted from writing about the subjects I had mentioned. "Completely prepos-terous," I had told him at the conclusion of his phone call.

I should note that I wasn't the only target of this particular public editor's ethical wrath. A few months later, Michael Gordon, the newspa-per's distinguished senior military correspondent, coauthor of two books about U.S. operations in Iraq, appeared on the Charlie Rose show and expressed, as what he called a "purely personal view," support for the military buildup then under discussion. "As a purely personal view," he said, "I think it's worth one last effort for sure to try to get this right, because my personal view is we've never really tried to win. We've simply been managing our way to defeat. And I think that if it's done right, I think that there is the chance to accomplish something."

As an expression of opinion, which Gordon made clear he was offering, this assessment differed little if at all from those in his books and in his published analyses in the *Times*. In his column on January 28, 2007, the public editor wrote that he had received "reader concerns" about Gordon's televised remarks and had raised those concerns with the editors. He then quoted Philip Taubman, the Washington bureau chief, as saying that "I would agree with you that he stepped over the line on the Charlie Rose show." The reporter's comments were "an aberration," Taubman said. "They were a poorly worded shorthand for some analytical points about the military and political situation in Baghdad that Michael has made in the newspaper in a more nuanced and unopinionated way. He agrees his comments on the show went too far."[12]

Not everyone agreed, however. Among the responses that appeared in the public editor's column the following week was one from a reader in Philadelphia that I will quote in full:

You and Philip Taubman, *The Times*'s Washington bureau chief, can only wish to be transmogrified through time into the old Soviet "minder" system. Anyone who steps out of line is watched and reported, then you apparatchiks gleefully slug back a vodka.

The screed against Michael Gordon was disgusting. We live in America. You have no right to chill him with your reproaches. If you don't want him to appear with Charlie Rose, then put it in his contract.[13]

Writing in the *Columbia Journalism Review,* Paul McLeary, senior editor of the magazine *Defense Technology International,* objected: "He said it in his book, his reporting for the *Times* has shown it, but he can't say it on television? . . . To not allow its reporters to speak out in public forums for fear of letting slip a less 'nuanced'— while still honest—appraisal of stories they know inside and out betrays a misunderstanding of the role of a journalist in the public realm."[14]

Evidently my editors agreed with me more than they agreed with Calame. I have to assume

the public editor was disappointed that I continued to cover the court and that nothing in
my assignment changed. (Neither did anything
in Gordon's.) But neither did any *Times* editor
come to my defense. "Not in the current climate," one explained to me. Defense was left to
letter writers; on October 15, 2006, the entire
public editor's column was taken up with letters
pro and con. "Linda Greenhouse is obviously in-
capable of distinguishing between facts and her
own strong opinions," one wrote.

But it was clear from other published letters
that there were two sides to this story, even if the
editors, usually so insistent that every story had
two sides, could in this instance see only one. "I
understand that *The Times* needs to be like Cae-
sar's wife, particularly these days, but how far
must journalists go to appear neutered?" wrote
a former chairman of the American Society of
Magazine Editors, who added, "As a retired editor, I'm free to say we're living in an Orwellian
world, but by the standards you describe, no
Times reporter is."

Although my editors' failure to take Calame's
advice about what to do with me spoke louder
than words, my disappointment in their lack of
a public defense was nonetheless acute. I prob-

ably should have felt more compassion for the editors, though. This wasn't the first headache I had ever given them. Seventeen years earlier, in the spring of 1989, I had joined some college classmates and a half million other people in a march for reproductive rights on the National Mall. It was an early experience of accidental activism, as well as an early encounter with journalism ethics under outside pressure.

The march was a huge event, highly publicized in advance. I turned down the organizers' offer of press credentials, because I didn't anticipate writing about it. I decided I would just go as a citizen. I later learned that not a few women at the *Times* in New York, including at least one in senior management, did acquire press credentials, regarding them as convenient cover. I saw no need to be coy about my plan to attend. In fact, I invited colleagues in the office, including my bosses, to join me. While no one took me up on the invitation, no one advised me not to go or expressed any concern about my participation. The march was on a Saturday afternoon. That night, there was a retirement party for a member of the *Times* Washington bureau. I arrived late at the party, announcing to the group, which included the bureau chief, as I walked in, "You guys missed a great march."

What happened next was that Leonard Downie Jr., then the managing editor of the *Washington Post,* heard that some *Post* reporters had participated in the march. Downie, a highly principled man who regards it as unethical for a journalist to vote, was dismayed. He and Benjamin Bradlee, the *Post*'s executive editor, announced that anyone who attended the march would be barred from "any future participation in coverage of the abortion issue."[15] My friends at the *Post,* trying to broaden their editor's perspective, mentioned that the *Times* evidently had no problem with my having marched. Instead of calming the waters, this revelation had the opposite of its intended effect. The *Post*'s media reporter was assigned to write a story and to call Max Frankel, the *Times* executive editor, to get his view on *Times* reporters participating in public demonstrations of this sort. (I'll digress here to note Downie's remarkable personal code of journalistic ethics, which he described on the occasion of his retirement in 2008: "I didn't just stop voting. I stopped having even private opinions about politicians or issues so that I would have a completely open mind in supervising our coverage."[16] Can this accomplished man really have believed that the highest and best use of a journalist's mind is to erase from it all judgment on, or even all response to, the times in which he lives?)

My participation in the march was news to Frankel—although of course it wasn't to Washington bureau chief Howell Raines, since I had told him about it in advance and been so public about it in the bureau, both before and after. Frankel called Raines and Raines summoned me to his office, letting me know in not quite so many words that the time had come to take a bullet for the newspaper and say that I was sorry to have made a mistake. I wasn't sorry, and I didn't think I had made a mistake. The person I felt sorry for was Raines, who was unable to summon the will to defend me to an executive editor who just as clearly was not going to allow himself to be seen as less ethical than his opposite number at the *Washington Post*. The rueful quote Raines gave to the *Post* reporter said it all: "This became what I would call a clarifying situation." The race was on. What evidently had not been a mistake when it happened was now, after the fact, a big one.[17]

Alex Jones, then the *Times* media reporter, was assigned to write the story, which appeared on

April 16, 1989, under the headline "Demonstration Renews Question of Conflict for Newspapers." The story asserted that while reporters' participation in the march had violated the conflict-of-interest policies at both newspapers, editors at both "believed the breaches were unwitting errors that stemmed from confusion over what was allowed and what was prohibited." Raines was quoted as saying that I had "identified" myself as having participated. "She now acknowledges that this was a mistake and accepts the policy," Raines said.

Jones didn't interview me for his story. Rather, as what he described as a courtesy, he called me to tell me what he was writing. He, too, was doing his duty, having evidently bought the party line with conviction. After listening to him, I asked him what he thought about the whole affair. "They should have taken you off the beat," he said.

"That's *your* opinion," I said, and hung up.

(I should note in passing that the episode received a great deal of media attention, not only domestically but also in Europe, where the notion that a newspaper should reveal no discernible political valence has always been alien. My favorite was an article in an Italian news magazine about the "enorme scandalo" in American journalism. It appeared under the unforgettable headline "La Marcia Proibita di Linda"—"Linda's Forbidden March.")[18]

A decade later, in retirement, Frankel wrote about the incident in his memoir. During his tenure as executive editor, "hardly a month passed" without a conflict-of-interest question requiring his attention, he wrote. By way of example, he said that "Linda Greenhouse, our brilliant Supreme Court reporter, failed at first to see why I objected to her participating in a Washington parade in support of abortion rights. She thought her anonymous appearance in a huge crowd was not the same as signing her name to a petition. I argued that it was no different than wearing a silent campaign button to a White House press briefing."[19]

Had Frankel and I argued? I don't even remember having a conversation. Is being one in a crowd of a half million marchers the same as displaying a political button in the intimate and tightly controlled setting of the White House press room? I wouldn't have thought so.

But details aren't what mattered in the episodes I have described, both of which have passed into journalism history and journalism school curricula.[20] Each stood for something deeper, crystallizing uncertainty and unease about the role of the journalist—indeed, of journalism—on our public landscape. The rapidly decentralizing world of nontraditional journalism has only heightened the concern. The conversation that Daniel Okrent hoped would occur has not taken place; in fact, the ranks have closed around the most reflexive response to the issue. In 2015, Diane Rehm, the seventy-eight-year-old host of a popular and assertively nonpolitical NPR talk show, ran into trouble for appearing on the cover of the magazine published by Compassion & Choices, an organization that advocates for aid in dying for terminally ill people. Rehm had watched her husband struggle for years with Parkinson's disease. By the time he was completely incapacitated, John Rehm wanted only to die, but under the law, no one could help him. So with the emotional support of his wife of fifty-four years, he stopped eating and drinking. Ten days later, he died. Rehm told her story to the *Washington Post,* where it appeared in an article that described her as "telling John's story at a series of small fundraising dinners with wealthy donors financing the [Compassion & Choices] right-to-die campaign."[21]

Elizabeth Jensen, NPR's ombudsman, immediately raised the question of what ethical rules should apply to Diane Rehm, who was employed not by the network itself but by one of its Washington, DC, affiliates. That distinction aside, should the rules that govern reporters also apply to talk show hosts? Evidently yes, in the ombudsman's opinion. And what were those rules? "My own view is that Rehm's participation as a celebrity guest of sorts at fundraising dinners for an organization that does extensive political lobbying, as compelling as her personal story is and as careful as she is being, is a step too far for someone associated with NPR," Jensen wrote on her blog.[22] NPR promptly revised its ethics policy to make clear that its prohibition against "political advocacy" will henceforth "apply to material that comes to NPR from independent producers, member station journalists, outside writers, commentators and visual journalists."[23] NPR announced that "to further avoid any perception of conflict, Diane has decided that after she honors her commitment to participate in two additional Compassion & Choices dinners this month, she will no longer participate in their fundraising events." "I think it's a good outcome," the NPR ombudsman said.[24]

Over the years, I watched with interest as my abortion march episode entered the realm of journalism mythology, changing shape along the way. Every spring for years, I received calls and letters from journalism students tasked with writing about it. Almost always, they believed that I had tried to keep my participation secret but had somehow been unmasked. It seemed impossible for them to believe that at the moment I actually marched, I had no reason even to think of hiding. The students had trouble grasping the fact that—as they certainly had not learned in journalism class—it had not always been the case that sanctimony was seen as the best defense against criticism. They listened politely to my correction of their narrative, but the facts seemed beyond the point. The point was to draw the line between the permitted and the prohibited. There had to be a line somewhere, didn't there?

2

Habits

Writing the Truth in the Age of Trump

President Donald J. Trump had been in office for a week and a day when a front-page *New York Times* story labeled him a "serial fabulist" who had spent the opening days of his administration unleashing "a torrent of bogus claims" and "reality distortions."[1] Strong words. Not half a year earlier, they would have been shocking words, even had the story been labeled "news analysis," which it was not. But the *Times* had crossed the Rubicon months earlier, using the word "lie" in the headline on the lead story in the paper of September 17, 2016, to describe candidate Trump's grudging recantation of his false claim that President Barack Obama was not born in the United States: "Trump Gives Up a Lie but Refuses to Repent."[2] And it would do so again just four days after the inauguration, reporting on the front page, "Meeting with Top Lawmakers, Trump Repeats an Election Lie" (that votes cast by millions of undocumented immigrants had cost him the popular victory).[3]

That the ever-cautious *New York Times,* considering itself the standard-bearer for American journalism, would take this step underscores the dislocation that the Trump candidacy and presidency has brought to the practice of mainstream journalism. Even before the president, on a visit to the Central Intelligence Agency during his first full day in office, declared, "I have a running war with the media"—and even before his chief strategist, Stephen Bannon, called the media "the opposition party"—major news outlets were wrestling with how to reconcile their obligation to call out Trump's falsehoods while adhering to the standard practices of journalism.

Those standards are the focus of this chapter. In order to appreciate the dimensions of the challenge the Trump administration presents to the mainstream media, it's crucial to understand how things were BT—before Trump. This chapter is a critical examination of the norm of "fair and balanced": where it comes from and where it has brought us—perhaps even to the age of Trump.

A minor episode early in the 2016 presidential primary season offered a glimpse of the journalistic struggles to come. No one knew it then, of course, but it served to frame the issue that the media would eventually have to confront on a nearly daily basis: what to do when a candidate for president, speaking on live television before an audience of millions, tells a lie. That the answer was neither immediately clear nor universally embraced demonstrates the powerful pull of habit, of the instinct bred in American journalists' bones that there must be at least two sides to every story and that to offer only one is to embark on a dangerous journey, away from the safe harbor of "objectivity."

The incident in the early fall of 2015—nearly forgotten today, in light of all that came later—offered a foretaste of what would come to be called fake news. At issue was video footage that an antiabortion group circulated purporting to show aborted fetuses being prepared at Planned Parenthood clinics for sale as tissue and body parts. During the second Republican debate, Carly Fiorina, enjoying some early buzz and seeking to prolong her moment in the sun, claimed to have seen on one of the videos an aborted "fully formed" fetus, "on the table, its heart beating, its legs kicking while someone says we have to keep it alive to harvest its brain."[4]

This was not a case in which the truth lay in the middle, between two extremes. Either the scene existed or it didn't. Had Fiorina "seen the footage," as she claimed, or—because it actually didn't exist—hadn't she?

It was a question the *New York Times* couldn't quite bring itself to answer. "Carly Fiorina Said to Exaggerate Content of Planned Parenthood Videos" was the headline on the newspaper's website. Note the ambiguous "said to"—did she exaggerate or didn't she? And doesn't "exaggerate" suggest that beneath some layers of overstatement lies a nugget of truth? The reader was left to wonder. Margaret Sullivan, the public editor at the time, took issue with the headline in a column entitled "Wanted: A Tougher Approach to Truth." She questioned Philip Corbett, the newspaper's "standards editor," who responded by defending "the neutral language of the *Times* news report." That left Sullivan unsatisfied. "The *Times* always serves readers best with reporting that pulls no punches," she observed.[5]

Other media, less bound to an internal rulebook and perhaps more attentive to what was unfolding in the political world, did a better job. "The footage Fiorina described does not exist,"

Time reported in a sophisticated article that not only unmasked the video at issue as a cut-and-paste amalgam of different events in different places; it also quoted doctors explaining that what was depicted was most likely the product not of an abortion but of a miscarriage of a pre-viable fetus.[6] One Associated Press story that received wide circulation was entitled "Fiorina Not Backing Down on Distortion of Planned Parenthood, Uses It as Campaign Centerpiece." The story reported that the scene Fiorina described (and that she dared President Obama and Hillary Clinton to watch) "does not occur in the videos."[7]

CNN provided readers with a link to an analysis by FactCheck.org, a nonpartisan organization that the Annenberg Public Policy Center had established in 1993 for the purpose of providing the media with fact-based evaluations of just such disputed claims.[8] The organization's report, entitled "Doubling Down on Falsehoods," revealed that the video clip of the fetus was actually stock footage that was unrelated to Planned Parenthood. The report concluded, "Fiorina is entitled to her opinion on whether Planned Parenthood deserves federal funding. But combining an unsupported anecdote with unrelated

footage does not add up to the scene she has repeatedly claimed exists on video."[9]

Definitive journalism of this sort, an explicit
refusal either to split the difference or to retreat
to the shelter of "he said, she said," should be so
routine and universal that there would be no
reason to highlight it as particularly notable.
Yet it's distressingly rare. I've been writing and
speaking on this subject for some time. In 2012,
Nieman Reports published my article "Challenging 'He Said, She Said' Journalism." I began
the article with a quote from a *New York Times*
story describing Fox News as "a channel with
a reputation for having a conservative political
view in much of its programming."[10] That almost
laughable construction insulated the reporter
from having to offer an informed characterization of Fox News on his own say-so. *A reputation?*
In whose mind and from what quarter? "What
was the purpose of that distancing phrase?" I
asked.

Examples continued to mount after the
Nieman Reports article appeared. In the fall of
2013, in the course of reporting a renewed
effort to bring immigration legislation before
Congress, a *Times* story observed, "The effort
comes just weeks after House conservatives

alienated many longtime supporters, including much of corporate America, by trying to block financing for Mr. Obama's health care law, a move widely blamed for the government shutdown."[11] *Widely blamed?* Why not just say what any informed reader knew: that the House Republicans' refusal to yield had *caused* the government shutdown?

Journalistic techniques for avoiding taking ownership of the content of an article come in several varieties. One is the type of distancing I have just described. Why was the reporter, or the reporter's editor, afraid to call Fox News a conservative channel? Why the reluctance to lay at the feet of the House Republicans responsibility for what they had done, and in fact had done proudly and openly? My guess is that the distancing constructions were the product not of conscious thought but rather of deeply ingrained habit, an instinctive aversion to any declarative statement or description, offered on a journalist's own authority, that might lead to a charge of partiality or "bias."

Another common distancing mechanism puts a characterization that the reporter fully believes to be correct in the mouth of someone else, perhaps an authentic expert or perhaps just someone with a title that suggests expertise, with quotation marks around the words. Mitchell Stephens, a journalism professor at New York University and wise observer of journalism's recent trajectory, calls this technique ventriloquism, a kind of laundering of the reporter's informed view of the matter—not infrequently, a better-informed view than that of the quoted source.[12]

Stephens is one of a number of scholars of contemporary journalism who argue that to be of value in the twenty-first century, journalism has to consist of something more than chronicling and fact-checking, more than what Stephens calls the age-old "noble obsession with accuracy."[13] Accuracy is of course essential, but it is not sufficient; there is no trick to quoting Carly Fiorina accurately in her remarks about the purported Planned Parenthood video. Rather, what the world needs is "wisdom journalism," which Stephens defines as journalism that "includes and even emphasizes informed, interpretive, explanatory, even opinionated takes on current events."[14]

A modern bible of journalism practice, *The Elements of Journalism: What Newspeople Should Know and the Public Should Expect,* which Bill Kovach—former curator of the Nieman Foundation and my former boss—wrote with Tom Rosenstiel, calls for a "journalism of verification" rather than a "journalism of assertion."[15] By this phrase, the authors mean that journalists have to take ownership of their material rather than simply redistribute content or repurpose facts. Neutrality, as such, is not a fundamental principle of journalism, they point out; rather, it can be a trap, an easy way out. The neutral voice, "without a discipline of verification, often is a veneer atop something hollow."[16]

(Margaret Sullivan's critique of the headline on the Fiorina story was not the *Times* public editor's last effort to call attention to this problem. A few months later, under the headline "Another Outbreak of 'False Balance'?," she criticized the paper's coverage of the controversy over childhood vaccines for failing to make clear that the benefit of vaccines is settled science, and for failing to discredit the asserted and disproven link between vaccines and autism.)[17]

After Robert Kaiser retired as managing editor of the *Washington Post* in early 2014, he wrote an opinion piece under the title "How Republicans Lost Their Mind, Democrats Lost Their Souls and Washington Lost Its Appeal." Linking to a recent *Post* story that reported without further comment that a Republican congressman from Texas, Randy Weber, had sent a tweet from the House floor calling President Obama a "socialistic dictator," Kaiser wrote, "One of my frustrations in recent years has been the journalistic conventions that can make it difficult to speak or write in a straightforward way about people such as Weber who make preposterous statements."[18] And Jeff Greenfield, reflecting on Jon Stewart's departure from *The Daily Show,* had this to say: "There are a lot of journalists who watch Stewart and envy the freedom he has. You can't go on television when you're a journalist and say, 'Senator X is a bald-faced liar.'"[19] Greenfield was writing in August 2015. Does his assessment still hold? Or are we all Jon Stewart now?

There is a puzzle, a disconnect between journalism practice and journalism commentary. Nearly all critics of contemporary journalism point to habits that disserve readers and viewers: imposing a false equivalency on ideas of unequal merit; using distancing techniques to create a semblance of neutrality; and taking the "view from nowhere," in the pungent phrase of the journalism critic Jay Rosen.[20] And yet these practices persist, even flourish.

For example, in the controversy about whether voters should be required to show particular forms of identification at the polls, there is really no debate about what game is afoot. In-person voting fraud of the sort that these new ID laws are purportedly designed to detect and deter is a nonexistent crime. It didn't exist before the 2016 election season, which saw a proliferation of voter ID laws in states with Republican governors and legislative majorities, and it played no role in the 2016 election itself.[21] (In July 2016, the United States Court of Appeals for the Fifth Circuit held that the strict voter ID law enacted by the Texas legislature discriminated against minority voters, observing that there had been only two convictions for in-person voter impersonation fraud in Texas out of twenty million votes cast during the decade that preceded the law's passage in 2014.)[22]

Even if fraud of this kind might theoretically occur, it would be a most inefficient way of trying to steal an election, one false identity at a time. And is it a coincidence that states with the most stringent ID requirements tend to be those with a troubling history of discrimination in access to the polls, or that the burden of coming up with an official birth certificate, or of traveling dozens of miles during the workday to a motor vehicles office when one doesn't own a car, falls most heavily on minorities and the poor? Conveniently enough, these are voters who, if permitted to vote, would likely vote for Democrats. The United States Court of Appeals for the Fourth Circuit emphasized this point in July 2016 when it struck down North Carolina's Republican-sponsored voter ID law, a law the court said targeted minority voters with "surgical precision."[23]

Trip Gabriel of the *New York Times* made certain that readers understood the background and actual intent of the voter ID laws when he reported in 2014 on Kris Kobach, the Kansas secretary of state. Kobach is the acknowledged godfather of the voter ID campaign and has recruited fellow conservative state officials around the country to climb aboard the voter ID bandwagon. Gabriel described Kobach as "an itinerant firebrand with a Yale law degree" who has had "an outsize influence in states as far-flung as Arizona and Alabama by raising alarms about illegal immigrants stealing elections, a claim without substance. . . . Although studies repeatedly show voter fraud of the type Mr. Kobach targets to be extremely rare, he has not toned down his message."[24]

And a few weeks earlier, another *Times* reporter, Timothy Williams, reporting on a voting-rights case from Ohio, declared flatly, in his own voice, "There has been virtually no in-person voter fraud documented in the country."[25] The public editor singled out this story for special praise, describing it as "some progress" in the battle against what she called "false balance" and adding, "This kind of thing doesn't happen every time it might."[26]

Indeed, it doesn't. A year later, as the 2016 campaign got fully under way, a page-one story in the *Times* reported on a new round of voting restrictions in Kansas. The story was structured in classic "on the one hand, on the other hand" fashion. It quoted "critics" who "assert that voter fraud is rare" and who charged that the Kansas law and others like it are intended to depress turnout among Democratic-leaning voters. And it quoted Kris Kobach, described only as "a supporter of strict voting laws," speaking in the law's defense. "This is a common sense way of ensuring that only U.S. citizens are able to vote," he said.[27] A *Times* reader with a less than perfect memory would have come away ignorant of Kobach's role in the voter ID campaign and could logically have concluded that both characterizations of the motivation for the law were equally plausible.

Another distancing technique is, if anything, more endemic and pernicious: the "he said, she said" format that in the name of "objectivity," "fairness," and "balance" reduces complicated, multifaceted issues to two sides and puts each side in the mouth of an advocate. ("We give *both* sides," was the boast of CNN in a 1993 advertisement.)[28] Aside from dumbing down and squeezing the nuance out of a complex debate, why is this common technique ("on the one hand, on the other hand") a serious problem? For one thing, there are often many sides to an important debate, not only two (and, of course, on issues of high moral salience—for example, torture, to which I will return—there may be a multiplicity of views but only one "side": it is wrong). For another—and torture is as good an example as any—presenting two sides without further explication or context, even or maybe especially when the quotes themselves are completely accurate, inevitably imposes a sense of balance or equivalence. If one side is correct and the other mistaken (for example, regarding childhood vaccines) or one side is morally insupportable (for example, arguing that torture is a valid technique in extreme circumstances), the resulting false balance or false equivalence can seriously disserve the reader—and society as well.

Thomas E. Patterson, Bradlee Professor of Government and the Press at the Harvard Kennedy School, points to a less obvious but equally regrettable consequence of "he said, she said" journalism. In his book *Informing the News,* he observes that while journalists may assume they are abiding by a professional code of neutrality in letting both sides have their say, what they are actually doing is something most journalists pride themselves on avoiding: deferring to power. "When a member of Congress tells a bald-faced lie and the journalist passes it along to the audience as a 'he said, she said' controversy, what except deference to those in 'power' explains the reporter's decision?" Patterson asks. "By conveying it, the reporter is complicit in the deception—the claim gets publicized and gains credibility as a result of being in the news." Inevitably, he concludes, "the objective reporting model absolves journalists of their part in the deception."[29]

When "he said, she said" journalism takes hold on a particularly contentious issue, it can distort or even shut down the kind of public debate that is critical in a democratic society. A recent example was the effort of states with antiabortion legislative majorities to invoke women's health as the rationale for imposing regulations on abortion clinics that the clinics predictably would be unable to meet. In fact, according to medical and public health organizations with directly relevant expertise, requirements for doctors at abortion clinics to have admitting privileges at local hospitals and for the clinics to be retrofitted as mini hospitals are unnecessary for women's health; by making abortion services inaccessible, these requirements actually threaten the health and well-being of pregnant women, especially those with few resources. These laws were a transparent subterfuge for restricting access to abortion to the maximum extent that a state could get away with, as the Supreme Court strongly suggested in June 2016 when it ruled unconstitutional a Texas law that would have had the effect of closing three-quarters of the state's abortion clinics.[30]

Not to acknowledge the actual context in which states are enacting access-restricting abortion regulations is to disable readers from drawing an informed conclusion about the current legal and political struggle over abortion rights. And yet this very failure was persistent throughout the trajectory of the case that led to the Supreme Court's decision. "Officials in Texas said that the contested provisions were needed to protect women's health. Abortion providers responded that the regulations were expensive, unnecessary and intended to put many of them out of business."[31] How was a reader to sort that out? And what was a reader to think of this line in a *Washington Post* article that appeared on the eve of the Supreme Court argument: "Abortion rights groups call these regulations disingenuous attempts to severely limit and ultimately end access to legal abortion, which these activists call one of the safest medical procedures available"?[32] The safety of abortion is a documented fact; the rate of major complications for abortions in the first trimester of pregnancy, when most of the nearly one million abortions performed every year in the United States take place, is 0.05 percent, making abortion one of the safest of all medical procedures. It doesn't take an "activist" to "call" it safe.[33]

In antiabortion states, abortion clinics are often the target of special regulations that don't apply to medical practices that perform procedures of equivalent or greater risk, a kind of "abortion exceptionalism" that is highly problematic as a legal matter.[34] In mainstream journalism as a whole, attention to context has, commendably, been increasing in recent years; in the words of Michael Schudson, a sociologist and leading scholar of the media, "Contextual journalism has settled in as conventional reporting's significant other."[35] But not when it comes to reporting about abortion. Perhaps there is an abortion exceptionalism in journalism as well: a special fear of labeling onerous and unnecessary health-justified regulations for what they really are, a kind of fog of war that envelopes the abortion conflict? Perhaps so, although it's a hard case to prove when a similar timidity seems to strike in so many other hot-button conflicts—voting rights, for example. The consequences of this kind of reporting are clear and disturbing. To apply Thomas Patterson's insight, simple parroting of the state's claims is a form of deference to power, lending the claims an undeserved credibility by pairing them with counterassertions and leaving the impression that there is really no way to sort out which side has the better of the argument. Maybe the earth revolves around the sun. Maybe it's the other way around. You decide.

"Objectivity excuses lazy reporting," Brent Cunningham, managing editor of the *Columbia Journalism Review,* observed in a 2003 essay in that magazine. "If you're on deadline and all you have is 'both sides of the story,' that's often good enough." Cunningham warned that objectivity "exacerbates our tendency to rely on official sources, which is the easiest, quickest way to get both the 'he said' and the 'she said,' and thus, 'balance.'"[36]

Given the prevalence of the criticism in the journalism literature, the lack of self-awareness in the daily life of the newsroom is surprising. Or maybe what it really reflects is a learned behavior of defensiveness. To quote Mitchell Stephens: "To work for a traditional American news organization today is to live not so much in fear that you'll be accused of bias, for of course you will be, but in fear that such an accusation might stick."[37]

Those who would use the media for their own purposes are easily able to exploit the opportunity offered by mainstream journalism's fear of not being "fair and balanced." As a candidate, Donald Trump understood this very well, knowing how disconcerting his tweets of "unfair" could be to editors and news directors who wanted to appear objective. Understanding the media better than the media understands itself is child's play for individuals and institutions specializing in providing "the other side of the story." Success in filling that role begets success. If such a person is quoted once or twice, there's a good chance of being quoted a third time or a fourth. Once that happens, that individual's role is institutionalized and the quote machine begins to operate almost by default.

One example of this phenomenon is the Criminal Justice Legal Foundation, an organization in Sacramento with seven employees, assets of $2.2 million, and expenditures of just over $600,000 a year, nearly all of it for salaries. In the nonprofit world, that's miniscule. The foundation describes itself as "the only public interest law foundation in America working full time to strengthen law enforcement's ability to assure that crime does not pay."[38] Kent Scheidegger, the Criminal Justice Legal Foundation's legal director since shortly after its founding in 1982, files friend-of-the-court briefs in occasional Supreme Court cases; so do many other, much bigger organizations. What distinguishes the Criminal Justice Legal Foundation is the role it describes in its federal tax exemption filing. "To provide the news media with timely and scholarly responses to claims made by anti-law enforcement advocates," the description begins.[39] At this, it has been spectacularly successful.

In the last ten years or so, Scheidegger and, occasionally, the organization's president, Michael Rushford, have been quoted in the *New York Times* more than seventy times. (A number of these were Associated Press stories, distributed nationwide and picked up by the *Times,* among other outlets.) To cite a few of the more recent *Times* stories: when a botched Ohio execution using lethal injection led to a debate over that method of execution, Scheidegger was quoted as saying, "Some of the witnesses say he [the defendant] was heard to make snoring noises. O.K., I've made snoring noises. What's not disputed is he got a large dose of sedative. We've gotten namby-pamby to the point that we give murderers sedatives before we kill them."[40]

Three days later, in a story about life sentences for juvenile offenders in the wake of a Supreme Court decision holding that such sentences could not be mandatory, Scheidegger was quoted as saying, "The Supreme Court has seriously overgeneralized about under-18 offenders. There are some under 18 who are thoroughly incorrigible criminals."[41] This article identified the Criminal Justice Legal Foundation as "a conservative group in Sacramento, Calif." The first story did not identify the organization at all.

When Governor Jerry Brown nominated Goodwin Liu, a Berkeley law professor, to the California Supreme Court, the Criminal Justice Legal Foundation, described as "a Sacramento group with a law enforcement focus," was quoted as objecting to the nomination because Professor Liu had criticized Samuel Alito's nomination to the United States Supreme Court.[42] An article about the shrinking numbers on death row evoked this response from Scheidegger: "The fact that the murder rate is down accounts for some of the softening. To some extent it's paradoxical: the death penalty brings down the crime rate and that lessens the need to impose the death penalty."[43] (Note that there is no evidence that the existence of the death penalty in fact "brings down the crime rate," and that this article simply accepted Scheidegger's assertion at face value and moved on.)

Scheidegger appears regularly in other publications as well. "It means we're going in the other direction," he told *USA Today* in December 2016 in answer to a question of how to interpret election results that preserved the death penalty in California and restored it in Nebraska. "The other side is not making progress. They are slipping."[44]

How does this small nonmembership organization (albeit one often described as "a group") manage to get quoted so frequently and paraded as the voice of law enforcement on so many different subjects? I asked several reporters how they had come to quote Scheidegger. "I called him after another potential conservative voice did not respond," one told me by e-mail. Another responded, "I reached out to him, and to several others. He was the one who called back in time for deadline, though—they only assigned me to do the story two hours before deadline. It's not a topic that I have written about a lot, so I had to rely on our previous stories to help me reach out to sources in a hurry."

This is not a criticism of Scheidegger or his organization. He is simply doing a job that the media rather desperately wants him to do. He adds something to these stories that looks like "balance." Because of the way the stories describe, or fail to describe, the Criminal Justice Legal Foundation, he also adds what would appear to any reader to be a voice of authority.

The need for the authoritative voice is another journalistic norm that is easily exploited by those who understand the media better than the media understands itself. One example is a law professor at the University of Richmond named Carl Tobias. Tobias, a prolific writer who lists his letters to the editor among the publications on his curriculum vitae, has been quoted in the *New York Times* more than one hundred times since he began teaching at Richmond in 2003. The range of his quoted expertise is impressive: from the punitive damages issue in the Exxon Valdez oil spill case,[45] to the fact that a football player showed up ahead of schedule to begin his prison sentence for promoting illegal dog fights ("It is an unusual move but not unprecedented," Tobias said),[46] to the filing of criminal charges for selling salmonella-infected peanuts ("Unusual," said Tobias),[47] to Volkswagen's hiring of Ken-

neth W. Feinberg to create a compensation plan
for owners of VWs with faulty emissions systems
("The point is to move away from litigation and
stop the hemorrhaging," Tobias said).[48] Tobias
also commented on whether the settlement of a
lawsuit against Trump University would hold up.
"A lot of work has gone into this, and people are
generally satisfied all around," he explained.[49]

Tobias generates many of these encounters
with reporters. I mean no criticism of him. I
don't detect any ideological inflection in his
comments. His only project, as far as I can tell,
is to get his name in the paper, and accomplishing
that goal by offering himself as a quotable voice
of authority on any manner of legal development is as easy as offering low-hanging fruit for
starving reporters to pick.

Journalism's flirtation with the form of authority, as in this instance, is harmless enough,
although laziness quickly becomes addictive. The
real problem is that it's too easy to slip from this
kind of benign laziness into a "he said, she said"
form that is not so benign, one that imposes a
judgment of equivalence on the forces contending
over issues of great moment. One particularly
notable example is provided by a Washington
lawyer named David B. Rivkin.

Rivkin, a lawyer in private practice with a specialty in oil and gas law, worked on domestic regulatory issues in the administrations of Presidents Ronald Reagan and George H. W. Bush. As far as is evident from his published résumé, he gained no particular national security experience during his federal government service. But in the later years of the George W. Bush administration, and continuing into the Obama presidency, Rivkin began appearing in articles about terrorism, and specifically about the detention of enemy combatants at Guantánamo Bay, invariably as a defender of whatever the Bush administration was doing or had done.

For example, when a federal district judge in Detroit declared that the Bush administration's warrantless wiretapping program was unconstitutional, Rivkin was given a platform in the *New York Times* account of the decision to say this: "It is an appallingly bad opinion, bad from both a philosophical and technical perspective, manifesting strong bias."[50] Rivkin was described in this story as "an official in the administrations of President Ronald Reagan and the first President Bush." There was no indication of what evidence he might have possessed that enabled him to accuse the judge, Anna Diggs Taylor, of "strong bias," or of what expertise permitted him to assess her "philosophical perspective."

When another federal judge ruled that some prisoners held by the United States at Bagram Air Base in Afghanistan had the right to petition for habeas corpus, Rivkin, identified as "an associate White House counsel in the administration of the first President Bush," was quoted as warning that the decision "gravely undermined" the country's "ability to detain enemy combatants for the duration of hostilities worldwide."[51] When details emerged about the type of interrogation the CIA had been conducting of suspected enemy combatants, Rivkin said, "Elaborate care went into figuring out the precise gradations of coercion. Yes, it's jarring. But it shows how both the lawyers and the non-lawyers tried to do the right thing."[52] He was identified as "a lawyer who served in the administrations of Ronald Reagan and George H. W. Bush."

While the stories I just described were all from the *New York Times,* Rivkin's journalistic usefulness was not limited to Times Square. When the Bush Justice Department's so-called torture memos came to light in 2009, the *Washington Post* quoted Rivkin as saying that the memos showed "careful and nuanced legal analysis" that had produced "eminently reasonable results."[53] Commendably, the *Washington Post* article described him as "a lawyer at Baker Hostetler who supported the detainee policies," thus neither endowing him with any particular expertise nor obscuring his position as an advocate (which might well raise the question of why he was quoted at all).

But that story remains an outlier. Rivkin even showed up on the *Times* culture pages, speaking critically about the film *Taxi to the Dark Side,* which portrayed the Bush administration's interrogation policies in a harsh light. "It's pretty clear that it's not policy and it's pretty clear that these things are prosecuted," said Rivkin, described as "a lawyer in the administrations of President Ronald Reagan and the first President Bush." The article continued, "Mr. Rivkin said the military's performance by historical standards has been quite good in the recent conflicts. 'In all the good wars,' he said, 'we have had some pretty bad records.' "[54]

As with the Kent Scheidegger quotes, I asked reporters how they had come to quote Rivkin. I quote here their e-mailed responses. "He reached out," one told me. Another said he had been referred to Rivkin by a conservative think tank. Another explained, "I called him, though I do notice that he markets himself fairly aggressively. I have quoted him a few times in the weird role of surrogate for the Bush administration. It was to the point that Bush administration officials would suggest him when they chose not to speak for themselves on Gitmo." Still another said, "I called him. I have known him for years. He is a good go-to proxy to articulate the Bush team's national security legal policy views."

From another, I received this response: "I called Rivkin, who has been defending the Bush policies for so long (especially interrogation) that he knows them as well as the human rights folks." Given that the article contained criticism of the policies, this reporter volunteered, "I thought it would be unfair not to make the opposite point."

While the examples I have quoted are all several years old, it's evident that neither Rivkin nor his usefulness disappeared with the end of the Bush administration. A *New York Times* article in 2015 quoted him on President Obama's use of executive orders. The president was stretching his authority in one direction and surrendering it in another, Rivkin observed, delivering this verdict: "The only unifying factor is political expediency."[55]

"Unfair not to make the opposite point." Where does this mandate for fairness and "objectivity" come from? Bill Kovach and Tom Rosenstiel, in their *Elements of Journalism,* omit both "fairness" and "balance" from their list of the ten principles of journalism. (The overarching goal of journalism, in their view, is "to provide people with the information they need to be free and self-governing.")[56] Why the omission? "Where is fairness? Where is balance?" they ask. Fairness "is so subjective a concept that it offered little guidance on how to operate. Balance, on the other hand, was an operational method that was so limited it often distorted the truth."[57] The Society of Professional Journalists dropped "objectivity" from its code of ethics in 1996.

Yet the roots are deep and can't be so easily extracted from journalism's soil. Adolph S. Ochs, the founding publisher of the modern *New York Times* (which really was a failing newspaper when Ochs bought it in 1896—its circulation was nine thousand, compared with six hundred thousand for Joseph Pulitzer's *New York World*), believed that a newspaper should "report all sides of a controversial issue, and let the reader decide the truth," according to a reminiscence published internally a few years ago.[58] Some journalism historians date the rise of objectivity as a norm to the 1890s, when, largely for marketing reasons, newspapers sought to appeal to as broad a group of potential readers as possible and began to draw a distinction between news and editorials. Elite newspapers sought to distinguish themselves from the "yellow journalism" of their cross-town rivals. More than simple economics was at work, surely. Journalists at this time tended to be better educated and began to think of themselves as professionals of a sort. Joseph Pulitzer endowed Columbia's journalism school in 1903, offering a path to employment through an elite credential. A journalism textbook from 1911 instructed students to "keep yourself out of the story."[59] As one student of journalism history reflected, "The act of taking oneself 'out' of stories begs the question: what is left in? What remains? The answer is that 'objectivity' remains, and the workers' voices are muted."[60]

"Workers," in this account, refers to the journalists themselves—newsmen, as reporters were collectively known until recent times. Indeed, Michael Schudson depicts the rise of the norm of objectivity as a managerial tool, "a kind of industrial discipline" that "enabled editors to keep lowly reporters in check." Publishers even invoked it "as a weapon against unionization in the newsroom (how could a reporter be 'objective' if he joined the Newspaper Guild?)."[61]

But if objectivity served only as a strategy for economic advantage or as a management tool, it's hard to imagine that it would have embedded itself so deeply in journalism's DNA as to become, in Schudson's words, "the chief occupational value of American journalism."[62] Certainly something else has been at work: a sense of professionalism, a way for journalists to distinguish themselves from press agents. This was no small matter as the objectivity norm took hold in the 1920s, when public relations was coming into its own as a profession, with better pay than could be found in many newsrooms. According to Schudson, "Objectivity seemed a natural and progressive ideology for an aspiring occupational group at a moment when science was god, efficiency was cherished, and increasingly prominent elites judged partisanship a vestige of the tribal 19th century."[63]

But the opposite of objectivity isn't partisanship, or needn't be. Rather, it is judgment, the hard work of sorting out the false claims from the true and discarding or at least labeling the false. It is calling public officials to account rather than simply—accurately—summarizing their press releases and public utterances. History provides abundant examples of the need for journalists to do the hard work, and of the consequences of failure. The run-up to the war in Iraq is one recent example. More than half a century ago, another was provided by Senator Joseph McCarthy and his reckless allegations of hidden Communists throughout the government. The late David S. Broder of the *Washington Post,* long regarded as the dean of Washington political reporting, recounted the episode in a 1987 memoir: "During his four-year rampage, McCarthy spread his accusations against a variety of government officials in speeches and hearings. It was all news by any definition—the words and actions of a prominent public official, raising charges of obvious import if they were true." Broder quoted senior correspondents of the day remembering how trapped they felt by the rules they had to play by. "Going 'beyond objectivity' meant going into dangerous, uncharted waters, where the safe and secure (if limiting) rules of the old tradition provided no guidance." Broder observed that "McCarthy understood newspaper deadlines and cycles and would supply fresh (or fresh-sounding) leads just when they were craved—and often when the fear of competition pushed newspapers to transmit and publish them before their accuracy could be checked." Edward R. Murrow helped bring McCarthy down with his *See It Now* documentary in 1954, but, as Broder pointed out, that came "late in the game" and after much damage had been done.[64]

A more recent test came over how to refer to waterboarding and other "enhanced interrogation techniques" used by the CIA on suspected terrorists in the months and years following 9 / 11. Waterboarding was commonly referred to as torture in news columns when it happened elsewhere. A study of four major newspapers published in 2010 by students under Professor Patterson's supervision at the Harvard Kennedy School's Joan Shorenstein Center on the Press, Politics and Public Policy was devastating on this point. Between 1931 and 1999, the study found, the *New York Times* published 54 articles that referred to waterboarding and characterized it as torture in 44 of them. But in 143 articles published between 2002 and 2008—in other words, when the United States was the actor in the spotlight—waterboarding was identified as torture only twice.[65]

The reaction to the report from the leaders of American journalism was fascinating. Bill Keller, then the *Times* executive editor, responded defensively that the study, "by focusing on whether we have embraced the politically correct term of art in our news stories, is somewhat misleading and tendentious." He explained, "When using a word amounts to taking sides in a political dispute, our general practice is to supply the readers with the information to decide for themselves."[66] At the *Washington Post,* which was also criticized in the study, Cameron W. Barr, the national security editor, said, "After use of the term 'torture' became contentious, we decided that we wouldn't use it in our voice to describe waterboarding and other harsh interrogation techniques authorized by the Bush administration."[67]

Arthur S. Brisbane, the *Times'* public editor at the time, revisited the issue a year later in the context of questions over whether torture had provided the intelligence that led to the killing of Osama bin Laden. The paper's news stories had avoided the word, while the editorials had used it freely. Readers were confused. Brisbane's column quoted Keller as explaining that in its news columns, the *Times* has not "banished the word 'torture,' but we are careful how we use it" in order to avoid the appearance of taking sides. The public editor urged the paper to be more forthright and avoid "the appearance of mincing words."[68]

It took years, but surrender finally came in mid-2014. Dean Baquet, who had become executive editor, announced on the newspaper's website that the *Times* had changed course, although he avoided blaming his predecessors for their stance. "When the first revelations emerged a decade ago, the situation was murky," he wrote. "The *Times* described what we knew of the program but avoided a label that was still in dispute, instead using terms like harsh or brutal interrogation methods." But with time, he continued, it became clear that in common usage, "torture" was not limited to a precise legal meaning but rather had come to mean "the intentional infliction of pain to make someone talk." In the future, the executive editor concluded, "the *Times* will use the word 'torture' to describe incidents in which we know for sure that interrogators inflicted pain on a prisoner in an effort to get information."[69]

It was the end of a perilous journey through the rocks and shoals of fairness and balance. In the end, adhering to the old rules came to be seen as more dangerous than crafting a new one. The moment still resonated for Baquet more than two years later, when he was asked to comment on the editors' decision to report Donald Trump's grudging concession that Barack Obama was born in the United States as the lead story under the eye-catching headline mentioned at the beginning of this chapter, "Trump Gives Up a Lie but Refuses to Repent."[70] It was "an extraordinary moment," Baquet said on a *Times* podcast, but not a difficult decision, because Trump "so clearly did lie" that "to have not called it a lie would have been false on our part."[71] By contrast, deciding to label waterboarding as torture was much harder. "We probably waited too long," he said.

Only plagiarism outstrips "bias" as journalism's cardinal sin. The problem is that while the definition of plagiarism is clear, bias is the most malleable of epithets, the boundaries of its definition potentially so capacious as to deter reporters and editors not only from making moral judgments but also from making any judgments at all. Recall the *Washington Post* editor Leonard Downie Jr.'s description of his own self-discipline: "I didn't just stop voting. I stopped having even private opinions about politicians or issues so that I would have a completely open mind in supervising our coverage."[72] While few journalists would or could go to such an extreme, Downie's position nonetheless stands as a kind of Greek ideal. I never heard anyone question, let alone criticize, it. I regard it as troubling, even frightening, to impose on journalists a sense of isolation from the civic life around them, from the very essence of citizenship.

If journalism is to consist of something more than entertainment and gossip—as it must—then its practitioners have to be something more than entertainers and gossips. They have to see themselves as participants in the ongoing democratic project of arming fellow citizens with the information they need to make informed choices. The American philosopher Alexander Meiklejohn maintained that this was the real meaning of the First Amendment, the "primary purpose" of which, he said, was to ensure "that all citizens shall, so far as possible, understand the issues which bear upon our common life."[73] It's hard for me to believe that journalists who self-consciously hold themselves apart from "our common life" are best equipped to serve that First Amendment role.

The great essayist Calvin Trillin expressed the dilemma posed by the norm of objectivity in the introduction to *Jackson, 1964,* a recent collection of his reporting from the peak years of the civil rights movement. "I was aware that I was expected to keep a certain reportorial distance," Trillin wrote. But that awareness presented a challenge: "I couldn't pretend that we were covering a struggle in which all sides—the side that thought, for instance, that all American citizens had the right to vote and the side that thought that people acting on such a belief should have their houses burned down—had an equally compelling case to make."[74]

Trillin described standing with Claude Sitton of the *New York Times* in the Trailways bus station in Montgomery, Alabama, as the first Freedom Ride bus was about to pull out, heading for Jackson, Mississippi. The two reporters stood there, "discussing whether being on the bus would make us participants rather than reporters. Finally, we decided that it was a public bus and we had a right to buy tickets. Also, other reporters were buying tickets. We got on the bus."[75]

Looking back fifty years later, Trillin found that "I'm no longer as certain as I once was about how bright the line was even back then." He ended his ironic reflection on the norm of objectivity with an anecdote from a fifty-year commemoration of the Freedom Rides:

When a session at that Freedom Ride commemoration ended with people linking arms and singing "We Shall Overcome," I made my usual quiet move toward the door. Suddenly, I felt someone link arms with me. Instinctively, I started to pull away while looking around to see who it was. It was an older woman in a wheelchair. Was I really going to wrest my arm away from an older woman in a wheelchair? I stayed. Then I joined in. It turns out that I still know most of the verses.[76]

Was Calvin Trillin biased? Yes, if the word means that he thought those whose struggle for equal rights he was chronicling were more deserving of victory than were their opponents. Would he have been a better journalist if he felt no personal stake in the outcome? I doubt it.

In 2009, a year after I left the *Times,* I began writing a twice-monthly opinion column for the newspaper's website. In this column, almost always focused on the Supreme Court, its members, and its docket, I expressed my opinion; needless to say, an opinion column without an opinion would be a failure. The column was often accompanied by a comment section, and I learned to expect that any particularly edgy column would attract comments like this one, evoked by a column posted on January 21, 2016, under the headline "Scalia's Putsch at the Supreme Court" (Justice Antonin Scalia was still on the bench, and the column took a critical look at his role in a recently argued case that threatened the future of public employee labor unions): "Interesting to see how stridently partisan Linda Greenhouse's views are now that she is a pundit. Are we really to believe that this partisanship did not impact her writings when she was a 'straight' news reporter? I know that liberals sneer at the notion of liberal bias but when reporters overtly reveal their liberal partisanship when they become pundits, it kind of makes those objections look like cognitive dissonance."[77]

Comments of this sort have escalated in number since the presidential election, especially in response to columns that are critical of the president. A column critical of the Senate Republicans' refusal to permit President Obama to fill the Supreme Court vacancy created by Justice Scalia's death elicited several such comments, of which this was typical: "Oh Linda, retire already. You used to be a reporter on the Supreme Court and now your [sic] an opinion writer. It is so evident now, that you [sic] reporting exhibited your left wing bias. Now it's evident for all to see . . . Shame, but now we know where you were coming from all those years as a 'reporter.'"[78]

"Bias" is a funny word. Once attached, it lasts long into the future, while also serving as a weapon that can be flung years or decades back in time. Maybe the commenter was actually familiar with my "straight" reporting work, although I doubt it. But now that he had me unmasked as an opinionated pundit, he felt free to impugn all of it. Underneath all that objective reporting for all those years, it turned out, there beat the heart of a liberal activist.

Dean Baquet maintained that the decision to call out Trump as a liar was easy. Maybe it was easy by the time he authorized "Trump Gives Up a Lie but Refuses to Repent" as the headline on the paper's lead story of September 17, 2016. After all, as Baquet explained on the *Times* podcast, Trump demonstrably did lie. Amplifying that explanation, Baquet gave an election-eve interview to the *Financial Times*. Asked about the headline, he replied, "We are used to warring philosophies, but this is different. This is a guy who makes stuff up. I am not opposed to his presidency, that is not my job. But my job is not to beat around the bush when a candidate lies."[79]

But Trump had lied before. He had been lying for months. (And he kept lying after the election, provoking such headlines as "Trump Falsely Says U.S. Claim of Russian Hacking Came after Election.")[80] In the beginning, it was not at all easy for the mainstream media to attach a label to what their reporters were seeing and hearing— just as it had not been easy to label Carly Fiorina's assertion on national television that she had seen a video that, on further examination, proved to be a deliberately misleading cut-and-paste job. As the campaign season gathered momentum, it became ever more challenging to report the new reality while adhering to the old norms. To watch coverage evolve was to see the norms bend under the strain and finally shatter.

I chronicle here what struck me as significant turning points in the coverage. The subject was usually, but not always, Donald Trump. In fact, one significant article appeared in February 2016, early in the primary season, and the target was Senator Ted Cruz. "Cruz Aides Spread False Report in Iowa That Carson Was Quitting" was the headline on a story by Trip Gabriel and Alan Rappeport. The story flatly labeled as "false" the e-mail and text messages sent by the Cruz campaign on the day of the Iowa caucuses to its Iowa supporters announcing the "breaking news" that Dr. Ben Carson "will be suspending campaigning following tonight's caucuses." Further, the story did not permit the "honest mistake" explanation offered by the Cruz campaign to stand unrebutted, noting that the Cruz messages continued despite an almost instant denial from the Carson campaign via Twitter and through reporters who were covering Carson.

The Cruz campaign then offered the *Times* reporters another explanation—that saying Carson would be "suspending campaigning" was not the same as saying he was dropping out, and that Carson had in fact "suspended" his campaign in the sense that he left Iowa after the caucuses and went home. "While perhaps narrowly correct," the reporters wrote, "it is largely understood that suspending a campaign means a candidate is quitting."[81]

But by far most of the increasingly skeptical coverage went to Trump. In December 2015, after Trump said that some sections of Paris were so full of radicalized Muslims that the police refused to go there, the *Times* story noted that "Mr. Trump's statement about Paris has no basis in fact: There are no districts there or outside Paris where the police have said they were unwilling to go."[82] The story earned praise from the public editor, Margaret Sullivan, as one of "some encouraging signs" that political stories wouldn't permit candidates to broadcast false claims. "Here's what makes readers justifiably crazy: false statements in news articles that are allowed to go unchallenged," the public editor wrote. "In any political season, it's especially important to counter those statements."[83]

Charges of outright falsehoods on Trump's part began to appear in the *Times* with some regularity as winter turned to spring, although not yet in the headlines. An article in late May 2016 about a baffling verbal attack on the chairwoman of the Republican Governors Association, Governor Susana Martinez of New Mexico, appeared under the bland headline "Trump Takes a Female, Hispanic Governor to Task." But the story itself was anything but bland: "He faulted her by falsely asserting she was allowing Syrian refugees to settle in the state."[84]

News stories began to describe him with adjectives that had rarely if ever been deployed in a reporter's own voice to describe a major public figure. On May 8, the morning after Trump won enough delegates to cinch the nomination, the lead story in the *Times* observed that "many Americans still cannot believe that the bombastic Mr. Trump, best known as a reality television star, will be on the ballot in November."[85] A story in August recounted Trump aides' inability to tame the candidate on social media, "where he continues to deliver outlandish attacks on all manner of adversaries."[86]

Those stories were not labeled "news analysis," and neither were a number of others that in an earlier day would have been so labeled for their edgy and opinionated tone. One example from mid-June, a page-one account of Trump's speech about terrorism and Muslims in the wake of the massacre of nightclub patrons in Orlando, is worth quoting at some length for context:

In his apocalyptic speech on Monday warning that terrorism could wipe out the United States—"There will be nothing, absolutely nothing left," he said—Mr. Trump substituted Muslim immigrants for the wolf pack. . . .

Exploitation of fear has been part of the American political playbook since colonial pamphleteers whipped their neighbors into a frenzy over British misrule. It took on new potency in the nuclear age with Lyndon Johnson's "Daisy" ad against Barry Goldwater in 1964 and Jimmy Carter's warnings about Ronald Reagan's finger on the button in 1980.

But Mr. Trump—who drew harsh condemnation from President Obama on Tuesday—has intensified the power of fear in presidential politics by demonizing an entire religious group. . . .

. . . Mr. Trump has committed himself to denigrating, if not steamrolling, the conditioned responses that have long served to help unite the country in times of crisis and offer Americans a chance to grieve and heal, and regain a sense of safety.[87]

The pointed headline on that article was "Old Political Tactic Is Revived: Exploiting Fear, Not Easing It."

My examples are from the *New York Times,* but the *Times* was hardly unique. An Associated Press story in mid-August that ran in newspapers nationwide under a Miami dateline began,

"Donald Trump repeatedly accused President Barack Obama of founding the Islamic State group on Thursday, refusing to take back a patently false allegation even when questioned about the logic of his position."[88] That the AP, among the most self-consciously cautious of all news organizations, would label a national candidate's statement as false without attributing that judgment to anyone was a clear indication of how much had changed.

Around that time, Jim Rutenberg, the astute media critic for the *Times,* offered a concerned but ultimately supportive appraisal of the sea change visible across the mainstream media landscape. Under the page-one headline "The Challenge Trump Poses to Objectivity," Rutenberg asked,

If you're a working journalist and you believe that Donald J. Trump is a demagogue playing to the nation's worst racist and nationalistic tendencies, that he cozies up to anti-American dictators and that he would be dangerous with control of the United States nuclear codes, how the heck are you supposed to cover him?

Because if you believe all of those things, you have to throw out the textbook American journalism has been using for the better part of the past half-century, if not longer, and approach it in a way you've never approached anything in your career. . . . You would move closer than you've ever been to being oppositional. That's uncomfortable and uncharted territory for every mainstream, nonopinion journalist I've ever known, and by normal standards, untenable.[89]

Rutenberg went on to discuss, and largely dismiss, charges of liberal bias raised by the candidate and his supporters and complaints that the media was not taking their grievances seriously. "This, however, is what being taken seriously looks like," Rutenberg wrote. For reporters to hold back on what they knew and observed

would also be an abdication of political journalism's most solemn duty: to ferret out what the candidates will be like in the most powerful office in the world.

It may not always seem fair to Mr. Trump or his supporters. But journalism shouldn't measure itself against any one campaign's definition of fairness. It is journalism's job to be true to the readers and viewers, and true to the facts, in a way that will stand up to history's judgment. To do anything less would be untenable.

This important article prompted more than two thousand comments on the paper's website. Predictably, some were critical: "The NY Times and all their minions wants to decide for us who to vote for because they have decided they know best." But many were supportive, expressing an "at last" sense of relief, including one that concluded, "Journalists also must remember that they are fellow citizens of their readers. Our fates are tied."

A candidate forum in early September 2016 sponsored by NBC News was a turning point of sorts. The moderator, Matt Lauer, was widely excoriated for his dogged pursuit of Hillary Clinton's e-mail problems while failing to challenge Trump's false claim that he had initially opposed the war in Iraq. While on the one hand, the negative fallout might be read as criticizing the moderator for a lack of old-fashioned "balance," by far the harshest criticism was aimed at his failure to call Trump out. "Any minimally prepared interviewer would have been ready for that claim," the *Times* television critic observed.[90] The notion that a debate moderator (the event was not formally a debate but rather a debate-like preliminary to the formal debates) has an affirmative obligation to challenge the participants' veracity is something new in American journalism. It's hard to imagine the old norm of passivity making a comeback. The expectation that candidates can use their free airtime to say whatever they want, and that any challenge will have to come from the opposing candidate, is likely to be a permanent victim of the 2016 campaign.

Did the campaign also kill the norm of "objectivity," of fairness and balance as the "chief occupational value" of American journalism? Not exactly. It could be argued that the campaign coverage exemplified—amplified—the faults of "fair and balanced" as the highest ideal. The filmmaker Ethan Coen, in a grimly amusing essay published the weekend after the election and entitled "2016 Election Thank You Notes," addressed "all our media friends" this way:

Thank you for preserving reportorial balance. You balanced Donald Trump's proposal that the military execute the innocent families of terrorists, against Hillary's emails. You balanced pot-stirring racist lies about President Obama's birth, against Hillary's emails. You balanced a religious test at our borders, torture by our military, jokes about assassination, unfounded claims of a rigged election, boasts about groping and paradoxical threats to sue anyone who confirmed the boasts, against Hillary's emails. You balanced endorsement of nuclear proliferation, against Hillary's emails. You balanced tirelessly, indefatigably; you balanced, you balanced, and then you balanced some more. And for that—we thank you.[91]

Did the *Times* publish Coen's essay with at least a shiver of self-recognition? I would like to think so.

But while calling Trump a liar in thirty-six-point type clearly broke a barrier, I'm far from certain that it established a new norm. The "Trump Lied" headlines, in the *New York Times* and elsewhere, provided a kind of emotional release for reporters and editors who had struggled for months to reconcile the world they knew with the world they were living in. Far from the action, I imagined the *Times* newsroom as I read the coverage, and I got a visceral sense of the high that comes from a deliberately transgressive act—a sense that was validated a week later when the *Times* ran a story entitled "A Week of Whoppers from Trump." Filling an entire page of the Sunday paper, the article listed the thirty-one "biggest whoppers" of the week. The reporters explained their project in this way: "All politi-

cians bend the truth to fit their purposes, including Hillary Clinton. But Donald J. Trump
has unleashed a blizzard of falsehoods, exaggerations, and outright lies in the general election,
peppering his speeches, interviews, and Twitter
posts with untruths so frequent that they can
seem flighty or random—even compulsive."[92]

A similar article appeared on the *Times* website after the inauguration. The White House
had issued a list of seventy-eight worldwide ter-
rorist attacks that it said had been inadequately
covered by U.S. mainstream media; the implicit
suggestion was that the media had made a delib-
erate choice to downplay the dangers of radical
Islam. "Our Articles on the Attacks Trump Says
the Media Didn't Cover" was the headline on an
article that listed each attack on the White House
list, with links to the news coverage of almost
all of them, most from the *Times* itself.[93]

How liberating that must have felt, I can only
imagine. And how hard to sustain. Skepticism
toward the new president's command of the facts
will undoubtedly continue, as it should. But an
unabashed adversarial stance in the news columns of a mainstream newspaper challenges the
very culture in which the current generation of
editors and reporters came of age. Twelve days

into the administration, Steve Adler, editor in chief of Reuters, sent a memo to the staff entitled "Covering Trump the Reuters Way":

It's not every day that a U.S. president calls journalists "among the most dishonest human beings on earth" or that his chief strategist dubs the media "the opposition party." It's hardly surprising that the air is thick with questions and theories about how to cover the new Administration.

So what is the Reuters answer? To oppose the administration? To appease it? To boycott its briefings? To use our platform to rally support for the media? All these ideas are out there, and they may be right for some news operations, but they don't make sense for Reuters.[94]

Michael Oreskes, a former *New York Times* editor who is now the top news executive at NPR, has strongly discouraged use of what is referred to at the network as "the L-word." Shortly after the inauguration, he explained his position to the NPR ombudsman: "Our job as journalists is to report—to find facts, establish their authenticity and share them with everybody. And I think that when you use words like lie, it gets in the way of that."[95]

And at least at the *Times,* the management was quick to make clear that the rules for individual conduct had not evolved to match the new climate in the news columns. The conflict-of-interest rule devised in the wake of my abortion-rights march more than a quarter century earlier still applied. In late December 2016, with Inauguration Day approaching, Philip Corbett, the standards editor, sent a memo to the staff entitled "Reminder on Impartiality." "As we cover the transition and the aftermath of the election, it's more important than ever for readers to see *The Times* as fair, impartial and independent," it began. "All of us in the newsroom—including those who don't cover politics or Washington—should do our part to protect that reputation."

That meant, the memo went on, that no one, no matter how remote their professional duties from the controversies of the day, should take part in any "activities that could raise doubts about *The Times*'s impartiality, including the planned women's march in Washington in January."

This makes little sense. Could the presence of a *New York Times* sports reporter or music critic standing with hundreds of thousands of other Americans on the National Mall to protest the inauguration of a president the newspaper's news columns have repeatedly labeled a liar really present a threat to the reputation of the *Times* as "fair, impartial and independent"? Or the presence of the newspaper's Supreme Court correspondent, for that matter? After proceeding to warn the staff against making contributions to "various nonprofit groups" that could "raise questions about our neutrality," the memo ended on a sanctimonious note: "We should remember that one of the best contributions we can make to our communities and our country is to protect and enhance the important work of Times journalism."

When I first read Michael Schudson's history of the origins of modern journalism ethics, I was skeptical of his assertion that the objectivity norm began as a management tool to control the behavior of the newspaper's employees. I have set aside my doubts: what was true in the early years of the twentieth century appears still to hold true in the twenty-first.

Old norms or new? Would my Radcliffe speech, with its objectively verifiable criticisms of Bush administration policies, be condemned as universally by the journalism establishment if I were still a reporter, giving a similar speech today to my fellow graduates about the policies of President Trump? Probably yes—but I'm not completely sure.

A month after the election, DeanBaquet was interviewed by Terry Gross on her NPR program, *Fresh Air*. The "Trump Lied" headline was a major topic of the hour-long interview. The *Times* executive editor said this: "I think that when we believe something is baseless, which is a real word, it's not an opinion. It is a word in the dictionary, and it means without any foundation in truth. I think if that word can be used very clearly and in this case accurately, I think that's journalism. And I think in fact to do the opposite would not be journalism. It would somehow be using language as a guard instead of using language to do what it's supposed to do, which is to tell the truth."[96]

3

Changes

Coming Home

I grew up in a newspaper-reading family. My mother was a New Yorker who had moved to the New Haven suburb of Hamden, Connecticut, as a bride and still needed her daily fix of the *New York Times*. Home delivery wasn't an option in Hamden in the 1950s, but it was possible to get the early city edition of the *Times* delivered in the day's mail. Every day when I came home from school, that morning's *Times* was waiting on the dining room table.

I can't say that I dropped everything to devour the day's paper. Nor were we the Kennedys, debating current events around the dinner table. But current events were in the air, and watching the nightly news was a family activity. Beginning in junior high school, I did spend a chunk of every Sunday afternoon with the Sunday *Times* (available at the neighborhood drugstore, where my father, a doctor, would chat with the pharmacist, who also served as Hamden's mayor, while I perused the latest movie magazines). My favorite section of the paper was the book review. I scanned it for books to add to the list I kept on my desk of those I planned to read someday; the *Tin Drum* was a perennial on that list, and I have yet to get to it. But my favorite part of the book review was the queries that people sent in about the origin of phrases from literature or lines from poems that they couldn't quite place. Readers were invited to respond with the answers. Taking *Bartlett's Familiar Quotations* off the shelf, I looked up every one and readily found the answers to a surprising number of the questions. I would mail my findings promptly on Monday, and once or twice I had the thrill of being the first with the answer and seeing my name in the *New York Times Book Review*—my first byline, and neither the editors nor the reader whose mystery I had solved knew that it belonged to a twelve-year-old girl.

Growing up, I knew only one lawyer. His name was Morris Gamm, Harvard Law School class of 1933. (I didn't meet a woman who was a lawyer until after I had graduated from college.) His office was down the hall from my father's medical office, and he was the go-to problem solver for everyone in town. He died in 2014 at 105, three years after the Town of Hamden, not for the first time, had proclaimed Morris Gamm Day.

So lawyers, as far as I could tell, were definitely people to look up to, and so were journalists. I knew only one of those, too: Charles Lenahan, the editor and publisher of the town's weekly newspaper, the *Hamden Chronicle.* People definitely looked up to Mr. Lenahan. Hamden was a sprawling suburb of forty thousand people, a collection of what had once been separate little villages, and there was no real downtown or center of gravity. The *Chronicle,* which regularly won regional newspaper awards, was what gave the town a sense of identity. Our high school newspaper, the *Dial,* was printed on the *Chronicle*'s press. As editor in chief, I made regular trips to the *Chronicle*'s building to hand Mr. Lenahan our copy, along with the marked-up pages that showed the layout we had decided on. In a cardigan sweater and with a pipe usually in his hand, he always seemed genuinely interested in how we were covering the goings-on in the town's only high school. I can't claim that he was in any sense a mentor. But he was an important man in town, engaged in serious work; by taking our work seriously, he elevated our enterprise and left a lasting impression on me.

Many small local newspapers are in the business of boosting and cheerleading, but Mr. Lenahan called it as he saw it. An example: In the spring of 1967 (I was away from home and in college by then), Senator Thomas Dodd of Connecticut was embroiled in a scandal that was to lead to his censure for diverting campaign funds for his personal use. An editorial that Mr. Lenahan wrote, entitled "Connecticut's Silent Press," asked why the state's newspapers weren't covering the situation. "Whatever the reason," he wrote, "the non-reading public of the state has been subjected to a remarkable example of non-reporting, of quite self-conscious evasion of an important public matter."[1] The editorial got quite a bit of attention beyond Hamden's borders. A few weeks later, Charles Lenahan died of a heart attack. He was forty.

If Mr. Lenahan was the first journalist I knew, John F. Kennedy was my first serious subject. I never met him. But I had a schoolgirl's crush even before he launched his presidential campaign; I had first noticed the handsome young senator while watching television coverage of the 1956 Democratic convention. After that, I read everything I could about him and his family. I clipped and saved articles from the news magazines. I started a Kennedy for President club at Michael J. Whalen Junior High School and distributed its newsletter, printing it on a mimeograph machine that my mother kept in the basement and used for the various civic associations she belonged to.

When Theodore H. White's *The Making of the President 1960* was published in 1961, I devoured it. Kennedy was in the White House by then, and what mesmerized me about the book was its account of the traveling press corps. These reporters were actually getting paid to fly around the country with my hero. It was their *job*. I can't say that Theodore White deserves sole blame for setting me on my career path. On the other hand, I can't say that he doesn't.

In describing John F. Kennedy as my first serious journalistic subject, I mean more than my junior high school mimeographed newsletter. On November 22, 1963, I was a senior in high school. I was devastated—plunged into mourning, dressing only in black for weeks, reading everything, saving everything—I was, after all, a sixteen-year-old girl in the full throes of heartbreak. A month after the assassination, in my capacity as editor, I took it upon myself to write an essay for the high school newspaper. I called it "The Longest Month," and Mr. Lenahan helped me position it on the front page of the *Dial,* surrounded by a thick black line. The essay was so sentimental that I won't quote it here. It ended with lines from a favorite and suitably mournful Emily Dickinson poem. Mawkish and over the top though it was, in its time and place it struck a chord, and one of New Haven's two daily newspapers, the *Journal-Courier,* reprinted it on Christmas Day under the headline "Hamden Senior Writes of the Longest Month."

As anyone who has ever been a teenager can imagine, seeing the essay in print in a real newspaper was a thrill and validation: my heartfelt, heart-rending words actually mattered to the adult world. And that was not the end of my journalistic relationship to John F. Kennedy. In the fall of 1965, I was a Radcliffe College sophomore, elected the previous spring to the staff of the Harvard *Crimson.* On one particular day, I was sitting in the back of a big Harvard lecture hall, pondering the approaching second anniversary of the assassination. The date loomed large in my mind. Why was no one talking about it?

I opened my notebook and, instead of taking notes in what I am embarrassed to recall was Professor Paul Freund's famous and wonderful undergraduate course in constitutional law, I wrote out my thoughts. By the end of the hour, I had finished something I dared to hope the *Crimson* might publish.

To say that I hadn't made my mark on the *Crimson* at that time is an understatement. I had been the only Radcliffe freshman with the nerve to enter and stick with the *Crimson* competition—the "comp"—the previous winter. The *Crimson* was a boys' club, a fraternity in all but name, complete with an open bar in the upstairs "sanctum," where a poker game was usually in progress. It wasn't all beer and poker; the editors (everyone on the staff was called "editor") worked as hard as they played, taking their journalism with great, even pretentious, seriousness. The comp was a trial by fire—trying to fit in, to have my work pass muster, to get the hidden rhythms of the place, the secret codes by which I was being judged. I was scared and insecure and exhausted much of the time, but determined and too stubborn to quit. Harvard had a rule in those days that required all student organizations to provide Radcliffe students with transportation back to their dorms after eight o'clock at night, so almost every night, and usually much later than eight o'clock, I took a cab from the *Crimson* back to the Radcliffe Quad. One night, late into the comp, I was standing in front of the *Crimson* building on Plympton Street waiting for my taxi when someone I knew from home, a Harvard student a couple of years ahead of me, came by. "Linda, what are you doing here?" he asked in surprise. "I'm comping for the *Crimson*," I said, and burst into tears.

That spring ended, blessedly, with my election. But it was obvious when the next fall came that election didn't automatically mean acceptance as a real member of the club. Acceptance had to be earned according to rules that remained obscure to me; clearly, what I yearned for was still out of reach. I walked to the *Crimson* after class that November day and typed up my Kennedy essay, handing it with some trepidation to the editorial page editor. The paper ran it as a signed editorial, entitled "November 22." This one, I will quote:

Last November 22 was the public anniversary—the end of official mourning, the disclosure of plans for a monument, the release of the official version of the story. This November 22 is the private anniversary.

We have built a wall of objectivity between us and that day two years ago—not consciously, but necessarily, because so much has changed. Comparisons between Johnson and Kennedy are rare now, not because we forget, but because the pace of events of these years gives such comparisons a tinge of unreality. The gulf is already too wide for us to say with any security what Kennedy would have done, much less thought, about the issues that concern us now.

The objectivity, though, goes just so far. We can hold a casual conversation about Kennedy for only a few minutes before the offhandedness becomes forced and the objectivity fades into an inarticulate and self-conscious reserve.

Part of the embarrassment is a reaction to the tasteless emotionalism that still surrounds the Kennedy name, a fear of being caught staring at the magazine covers with their sometimes sensational, sometimes only painfully sentimental headlines which still confront us in the Square.

But that is not all of it, for while the volume of vulgarity has decreased since the public anniversary, our embarrassment has not. The embarrassment is due rather to an admission which we are not yet

quite ready to make: For us there will never be another Kennedy.

For he was the matrix of our political awakening.
We were in high school when he became President;
half of us were still in high school when he died. He
was our candidate—the first national figure whose
emergence we could watch and whose victory we
could celebrate as our own. Only once in a lifetime
is it possible to feel the first tremendous excitement,
to give oneself completely—as another generation
gave itself to Roosevelt, perhaps—to a figure as remote as the President of the United States.

Because once it is over things can never be so
simple again. Kennedy was, in a real sense, all of
politics to us then. The questions were few and the
answers were easy, because he was the ultimate standard. There will be other Presidents who we will
support on their paths to the White House, but
never again will we feel the personal closeness to the
center, the excitement that we did then; we feel old
now—we have outgrown our political youth and
read now about politicians instead of heroes and
write papers on the complexities of power.

Had Kennedy lived to serve his full term and
then retired, the same thing would have happened;
it is inevitable. But his death stands as a line of

demarcation in our political maturity: before it, we felt a security, an optimism, and a faith that in the end, every problem could be solved by a man who was uniquely ours.

We long in secret to recapture that faith; we know that it was naïve and we blush for it. And, thinking back on this second anniversary to those days of faith, two years seem like a long, long time.

I believe that was the last time that I had occasion to write about John F. Kennedy. I had written the essay, really, for myself, not with any bigger goal in mind. I was just grateful that the senior editors had been willing to print it. But its effect on a community that saw itself as uniquely associated with Kennedy was immediate, and its impact on my own sense of place in that community was to prove lasting. It signaled my acceptance as a full-fledged member of the *Crimson,* even as a voice of student journalism at Harvard. I received fan mail from Harvard administrators, pats on the back from the editors. "You have soul to burn," one *Crimson* senior who had never so much as deigned to speak to me wrote, in the idiom of the day, in the comment book in which staff members critiqued and, rarely, praised one another's work.

My favorite response to the essay came from a member of the Harvard class of 1924, who wrote not to me but to Don Graham, the *Crimson*'s president. "Dear Donald Graham," Harry Eldridge wrote. "The editorial in the November 22 issue of *The Crimson* is very fine and thoughtful. It has a purpose for wider circulation. I roomed in college with the president and manager of *The Crimson*. It carries on a splendid reputation. That the editorial was by a female correspondent intrigues me."

Not too many people in those days were intrigued by female correspondents. I was the Harvard stringer for the *Boston Herald,* which regularly printed my accounts of student antiwar protests and other newsworthy Harvard events in 1967 and 1968, usually without changing a word. But the *Herald* didn't offer me an interview when I applied for a real job. Neither did the *Boston Globe*. Looking through some old files recently, I found polite but firmly discouraging rejection letters from places I can't even remember having applied to. The letters didn't say so—Title VII of the Civil Rights Act of 1964 was now the law, prohibiting sex discrimination in employment—but it was clear that women weren't wanted in the newsroom.

Through the *Crimson* network, I learned of a potential, unadvertised job. James Reston of the *New York Times,* one of the most respected political columnists of the day, had his own internship program in his office in the *Times* Washington bureau, roughly modeled after a Supreme Court clerkship. He would hire a fresh college graduate to spend a year with him, doing research for the column and generally serving as a helpmate and sounding board. The year almost always led to an entry-level position on the reporting staff. Scotty, as he was known, had never hired a woman. But the Vietnam draft was on, and one or two clerks had been drafted out from under him. That opened the mind of this old-fashioned father of three sons to the prospect of hiring a woman.

Shortly after hiring me, Reston himself got a new job. Turmoil in the executive suite had led Arthur O. Sulzberger, the *Times* publisher, to install Reston, in whom he had complete trust, as executive editor while things sorted themselves out. That meant a move from Washington, where I had greatly been looking forward to living and had already rented an apartment, to New York, where I hadn't even thought to look for a job. Knowing that the internship lasted only for a year, and having no particular expectation that the *Times* would hire me when my year was up, I assumed my stay in New York would be temporary. It took me ten years to get back to the Washington bureau, then as the paper's Supreme Court correspondent.

As executive editor, Scotty Reston had a full complement of adult assistants and didn't really need my help. That left me largely free to write, and to peddle my stories to the editors of any section of the paper that might print them. I wrote about thoroughbred horse breeding—a subject about which I actually knew quite a bit—for the sports department and its wonderful, avuncular editor, Jim Roach, and I wrote about bathing suits—about which I knew very little—for the fashion page and its fascinating and breathtakingly fashionable editor, Charlotte Curtis. With a New York City guidebook and a subway token, I explored and wrote about obscure outer-borough neighborhoods to which real *New York Times* reporters rarely ventured.

New York magazine was a new publication in the city, living off freelance contributions. I wrote a string of articles for *New York,* including a portrait of the Parkchester neighborhood in the Bronx that the magazine displayed prominently and that received some notice. A. M. Rosenthal, an authoritarian figure newly installed as managing editor of the *Times,* stopped by my desk one day and asked why I was writing those stories for *New York* magazine and not for the newspaper. He had never spoken to me before, and I was terrified. The fact was that while the *New York* magazine stories carried my name, the *Times* didn't give bylines to lowly news clerks like me. "I'm doing it for the byline," I stammered. It happened to be precisely the right answer. Abe Rosenthal perched on the corner of my desk and told me about his days as the City College stringer for the *Times* and about how much it had meant to him to get his first *New York Times* bylines. By the end of what was essentially a one-way conversation, I felt I had passed some sort of test. When my Reston year was up, I received a try-out spot on the metropolitan staff. Within a few months, I got my first byline. I remember the story as having been about an early snowfall. There was no ceremony attached to the occasion. I was twenty-two years old, and all I cared about was what was going to happen next, whatever that might turn out to be.

No one knew it then, of course, but I had been admitted to a profession and an industry that by the end of my career would face profound and disruptive change. My desk near the back of the open, block-long newsroom gave me a geographic vantage point on a system that had been largely unchanged for decades. Nearly all the people seated at row after row of adjoining desks were white and male. Quite a few were veterans of World War II. Some of the finest writers on the staff did not have college degrees. Deadlines were dictated by a strict production schedule, based on the time the presses deep in the basement needed to start running: what looked from the outside like an office building was in many ways really a factory, in the heart of Manhattan. Seven o'clock was the deadline then for stories aimed at the city edition, which hit newsstands in Times Square at about the time the Broadway theaters let out. As deadlines approached, the smoke-filled air of the newsroom rang with the musically syncopated cadence of "co-py!" summoning copy boys who would promptly appear to take the "ten-part book" from the reporter's hand. These were ten sheets of typing paper interlaced with carbon paper and bound together at the top. These were what reporters, using the manual typewriters bolted to each desk in the newsroom, composed their stories on, one "take" at a time if it was a deadline story. The copy boy handed one sheet back to the reporter, keeping the other nine for eventual distribution to the various parts of the editing and production process.

There were, of course, no cell phones—finding a working phone from which to call in a story to the men who took dictation in the "recording room" was a major challenge in an unfamiliar neighborhood—and no fax machines. When I was in the state capital bureau in Albany and an editorial writer in New York needed to see a decision from the New York Court of Appeals, the state's highest court, a member of our bureau would pick the opinion up from the courthouse and take it to the Trailways bus station for the 150-mile journey south. Hours later, or maybe not until the next morning, the package could be retrieved from the Port Authority bus terminal a few blocks from the *Times* building. Events unfolded then as quickly as they do now, certainly, but the ability to tell the world about them was sharply constrained by the limitations of technology. Somehow the world kept on spinning without a constant and instantaneous flow of information.

In the absence of cell phones, to be out of the office was to be out of pocket: not a good thing from an editor's point of view. I learned that lesson in one of my first assignments as a brand-new general-assignment reporter. New York City's buses were converting to an exact-change system. On the first day of the changeover, the metropolitan desk deployed reporters all around the city to see how riders were taking to the new system. I was assigned to ride the buses in Queens. I took this assignment seriously to mean all of Queens. Queens is a large borough, completely unknown to me at the time except as a name on the map. I set out early in the morning, taking the F train a few stops into the borough and catching the first bus that came along. I took detailed notes of the interactions between the bus drivers and the riders. Then I caught a bus going in a different direction, and did the same thing. This continued well into the afternoon. I had a notebook full of anecdotes by the time I arrived back in the office to compose a memo for the reporter on the rewrite desk who would actually write the story. My confidence that I had done a commendable job was quickly shattered when an assistant metro editor barked, "Where the hell have you been all day?" From this episode, I learned two lessons. When out of the office for any extended period, even while doing the precise job that has been assigned, find a pay phone and check in with the office at least every two hours. And most important, understand the nature and scope of the assignment. While by mid-afternoon I could have produced a short book on the nature of public transportation in the borough of Queens, all the rewrite reporter needed and wanted from me was a quote or two to show that the *Times* had indeed been on the scene in every borough. One bus ride of a few blocks would have sufficed. Clearly, just as in my early days on the *Crimson,* I had a lot to learn.

A number of my assignments were a bit more engaging, even before I was deemed worthy of a byline. One would have a lasting impact on my professional life. I was assigned to cover a news conference convened to announce the filing of a lawsuit challenging the constitutionality of the New York law that made abortion a crime. Every state had such a law, although California's had recently been invalidated by the California Supreme Court, and a federal judge had expressed doubts about the constitutionality of the law in the District of Columbia. I knew very little about abortion except as a terrifying fate that awaited unlucky teenagers and college girls. I knew just as little about law. But the lawyers did a good job of explaining the basis for the case they were bringing on behalf of four doctors. One of the lawyers, Roy Lucas, two years out of New York University Law School and still in his twenties, did most of the explaining. New York's criminal ban on abortion, which dated to 1828, provided an exception if terminating the pregnancy was necessary to save a woman's life. The suit challenged this provision as unconstitutionally vague, Mr. Lucas explained, because doctors had no way of knowing whether the exception applied only if a woman would "die the next day, or whether she will have two days taken off her lifespan."

In addition, the plaintiffs charged that the law violated both a doctor's right to practice medicine according to the highest standards and a patient's right to safe and adequate medical advice and treatment. Finally, the complaint alleged that the law violated the constitutional right to privacy as defined by the Supreme Court four years earlier in *Griswold v. Connecticut,* a landmark case that established a constitutional right to contraception.

I was unaware of the *Griswold* case and had never heard abortion openly discussed, let alone in such interesting and challenging terms. My

story ran on October 1, 1969, under the headline "State Abortion Curb Challenged in Suit as
a Violation of Rights." The story, without a byline, began, "A suit was filed in federal court yesterday for an injunction against the enforcement
of the state abortion law on the grounds that it is
unconstitutionally vague and denies fundamental
rights to women and their doctors."

The story got the attention of the *Times*
Sunday magazine editors, who asked if I would
write a magazine article on the issues raised by
the lawsuit. This was a request, not an assignment: in those days, reporters who wrote for the
magazine did so on a freelance basis, on their
own time for extra pay. I couldn't take time off
from my day job on general assignment, so I
worked feverishly nights and weekends. I talked
to everyone involved in what were in fact four
separate lawsuits. The lawyers took time with
me, patiently explaining the roots of the constitutional framework they were seeking to establish. The young lawyer in the state attorney
general's office tasked with defending the state
law explained why, in the state's view, the *Griswold* precedent was inapplicable: preventing a
pregnancy and deliberately ending one were not
comparable acts.

The magazine's editors were surprised when I turned in my article within weeks. They changed almost nothing and quickly scheduled it for publication. It appeared on January 25, 1970, under the provocative headline "Constitutional Question: Is There a Right to Abortion?" It had a byline. The article explained that abortion reformers were turning to the courts because efforts at legislative reform had failed—including, stunningly, in New York the previous spring:

More important than the change of tactics is the change of philosophy that underlies the new abortion-reform movement. The reformers no longer claim that the states, basically correct in regulating abortion, are simply too rigid in the way they apply this power. Now, they are seeking to establish abortion as a positive legal right, like the right to free speech or the right to be secure against unlawful search and seizure, protected by the United States Constitution against interference by the state on any but the most pressing grounds. If they succeed, it is just possible that there will not be an abortion law left standing in any state by the end of this year.

The lawsuit itself, *Abramowicz v. Lefkowitz,* never came to fruition; within months, the New

York Legislature reversed course and repealed the nineteenth-century law. But while the lawsuit was moot, the article was not. It resonated widely as the first time a mass-readership magazine framed the case for a constitutional right to abortion. Litigation continued around the country. Three years later, almost to the day, the Supreme Court decided *Roe v. Wade.*

I was off general assignment by then, assigned as the sole occupant of the newspaper's suburban bureau in White Plains, the county seat of Westchester County. The Westchester beat was a lonely trial at first. I knew no one. The *Times* gave me a car, but, with a sense of direction that has not improved with age, I was often lost somewhere among the county's forty-eight municipalities, covering 450 square miles. I rarely received assignments and even more rarely received any guidance about what the metropolitan desk wanted from Westchester. Keeping my apartment on Manhattan's Upper West Side, I had a thirty-mile commute each way. Once I arrived at the White Plains bureau, which I shared with two advertising salesmen and their secretary, it was up to me to fill my days and produce stories that the paper would print.

In more than three years working in Westchester, I made lifelong friends and almost met
my future husband, Eugene Fidell, who was part
of the legal team representing Consolidated Ed-
ison in a nuclear power plant licensing proceeding that I covered. Our paths didn't cross
then, any more than they had crossed during the
three years when we were both students at Harvard, Gene at the law school and I at Radcliffe.
(We finally met in Washington, DC, in 1979.)
Westchester provided a steady diet of decent
stories, including a running controversy over a
state agency's effort to persuade nine nearly all-
white towns to accept a modest quotient of
subsidized housing that would, by implication,
introduce a measure of racial diversity. By the
time I left the Westchester beat in the spring of
1973, none of the proposed homes had been
built.

At the time, the radio station the *Times* owned,
WQXR, ran a nightly preview of the next day's
stories, with Clifton Daniel, a former managing
editor, acting as host and interviewing the reporters whose stories the program featured that
night. He called once and suggested that we do
a dry run before the taping. I don't remember the

story (probably the nine towns), but I do recall the conversation. He posed his first question, and I began my answer: "Well, Mr. Daniel . . ." He interrupted: "No, no, *on the air* call me Clifton."

I received so little feedback from the editors, whom I saw rarely, that I eventually summoned the courage to make an appointment to go into the main office and talk with Arthur Gelb, the metropolitan editor. "How do you think I'm doing?" I asked him. "Do you think I'm a good writer?" "Not particularly," he replied. It was the longest conversation I ever had with Arthur Gelb, who later became managing editor. He was a legendary figure in American journalism, and when he died at ninety in 2014, I was interested to learn from his obituary that he was "known for nurturing young talent."[2]

I did have another encounter with law while on the Westchester beat. In 1965, there had been a devastating fire at the Jewish Community Center in Yonkers. Nine children and three adults had died, and arson was suspected. The suspicion fell on a sixteen-year-old boy, Thomas Ruppert, who was working at the center in an after-school maintenance job. The police interrogated him intensively over a thirty-three-day period until he confessed. He was convicted and sentenced to life in prison. An appeals court threw out the confession and ordered a new trial because the police had not given the boy the warnings required by the Supreme Court's *Miranda* ruling, which was decided shortly after his indictment on charges of arson and murder. The question at the hearing I covered in 1970 was whether the prosecution could introduce at the new trial a second confession the boy had made to the Jewish center's director, or whether that confession would also have to be suppressed because the director and the police had worked so closely together that the director had effectively acted as an agent of the police. (The state's highest court ultimately ruled that the second confession had been coerced and, because the state had no other evidence of guilt, the court dismissed the charges.)

Tommy Ruppert's lawyer was a sole practitioner named Eleanor Jackson Piel who undertook to teach me some law. The *Miranda* decision had passed me by in 1966, when I was paying attention to the war in Vietnam and the war in the streets rather than to the Supreme Court's shifting view of compelled self-incrimination. Eleanor Piel dressed impeccably and lived grandly in a Fifth Avenue penthouse with her husband, Gerard Piel, a descendant of the Piels beer family and the longtime publisher of *Scientific American*. She was in her early fifties when we met. She had been the only woman to graduate law school with the class of 1943 from the University of California at Berkeley, and she continued to practice criminal defense law into her nineties, specializing in death penalty appeals. Her devotion to the cause of her downtrodden clients was absolute, and she defended Tommy Ruppert with passion and creativity. We spent hours discussing criminal law.

Most of my college friends and classmates had gone on to graduate study of some kind, and at times I felt a bit defensive about having gone straight into the workforce. But I was learning all the time, and a good deal of it was law related: constitutional law from the plaintiffs' lawyers in the abortion case, nuclear regulatory law for the power plant hearings, zoning law for the nine-towns controversy, and now a private tutorial in criminal law from this fascinating woman.

One of my greatest pleasures at the Harvard *Crimson,* one that helped shape my resolve to pursue a career in journalism, had been the ability to call famous Harvard professors on the phone or knock on their doors, not as a mere undergraduate but as a Harvard *Crimson* editor. Approaching professors as a journalist brought great rewards. I spent days with the sociologist David Riesman, author of the famous book *The Lonely Crowd,* for a *Crimson* feature on his life's work. One Sunday afternoon, I called John Kenneth Galbraith with a question about some economic development, and he invited me to his house to discuss it further. Harvard was not an intimate place, and student-faculty contact outside a formal academic setting was infrequent. I was one of five hundred students in the introductory economics course that Professor Galbraith supervised. Chatting with him in his comfortable living room on a Sunday afternoon was heady and seductive. These experiences were also extremely useful. In my early months at the *Crimson,* I would stare at the telephone, summoning the courage to call one of these academic giants, afraid of stumbling over my own name. I learned to suppress my nerves and keep a conversation going with just about anyone. Soon enough, I would be taking those skills to a new arena.

In the spring of 1973, I was summoned back from Westchester and assigned to the night rewrite desk; the editors needed to make room in White Plains for a foreign correspondent who was coming home and for whom the Westchester beat offered a comfortable preretirement post. Night rewrite was an unglamorous although respected assignment. It prized speed and a certain amount of self-confidence in handling fast-breaking stories, which could be a fire in Brooklyn or a coup in a foreign capital (the overthrow and murder of Salvador Allende in Chile happened on my watch, and I had an hour or so to write Allende's obituary, since there was none on file). One requirement for election to the *Crimson* had been the ability to write a page of news copy, from a standing start, in five minutes. It was a skill that not many *Times* reporters had acquired, and it served me well.

Some days, my night rewrite shift began at two o'clock in the afternoon and ended at nine thirty at night. On other days, it began at four o'clock and ended at eleven thirty. I usually worked one weekend day and had one weekday off. These free hours were useful, because I had some unfinished business to attend to. The U.S. Military Academy at West Point, although across the Hudson River from Westchester County, was considered part of the Westchester reporter's territory, and I had made several visits there, mostly to cover the cheating scandals that erupted periodically. On one such visit, I got an amazing tip. There was a cadet about to graduate who had spent the final nineteen months of his four years at West Point ostracized by all the other cadets. They refused to sit with him at meals or even talk to him. They believed that he had cheated on a test by continuing to write after time was up. He denied it. He had been brought up on charges before the cadet-run honor board, but the charges were dismissed for improper command influence after a supervising officer had communicated his opinion to the honor board that the cadet was guilty. Furious at this turn of events, the corps of cadets voted to impose an unofficial but officially tolerated punishment known as "the Silence." Most cadets facing such treatment quietly resigned. But this kid, James Pelosi, son of a World War II bomber pilot, stuck it out and was about to be commissioned as a second lieutenant. I could hardly believe what I was hearing from the law student who called me, a former military officer who had learned about what was happening from a contact at West Point and who was now writing a law review article on the legal implications of the Silence.

I got in touch with Jim Pelosi, interviewed him and his family, and was determined to tell his story. After leaving the Westchester bureau, I kept working on it. I didn't tell the editors anything about it; I think I was afraid that since West Point was no longer part of my beat, they would order me to stop. My idea was to get assigned to cover the West Point graduation and then, in the following day's paper, the story that would appear under my byline would not be the conventional graduation story but the story of the Silence and of the young man who had endured it. I got the assignment. The day before the graduation, I handed my finished story to Marvin Siegel, one of the assistant metropolitan editors who had always been friendly to me. Then I went home.

A few hours later, Marv Siegel called me in a state of high excitement. He loved the story. All the editors loved the story. My plan had worked. I drove up to West Point the next morning and, with my press credential, sat in the stands to witness the graduation. The story ran on page one on June 7, 1973, under the headline "Silent Agony Ends for Cadet at Point." Datelined West Point, New York, it began, "James J. Pelosi was graduated from the United States

Military Academy here today, more than a year and a half after he was officially 'silenced' by his fellow cadets." It told Jim Pelosi's story, amplified by entries from a diary he had shared with me. It recounted the history of the Silence, which forty years earlier had been imposed on a black cadet, Benjamin O. Davis, simply because of his race. Like Cadet Pelosi, Cadet Davis had endured it, in his case for all four years of his time at West Point. He went on to become a lieutenant general in the air force.

The impact was certainly greater than anything I had written during my five years at the *Times,* and probably greater than any single story I wrote afterward. There were immediate demands for congressional hearings, and general outrage that the military academy could have taken a hands-off attitude and tolerated such behavior. A television producer called me. A television drama about the episode was in the works. Would I like to have some involvement in the project? I was feeling a little overwhelmed, and I was naïve. I didn't think the editors would let me take time off from night rewrite to work on a movie, and I didn't want to ask them. A year and a half later, *The Silence* was broadcast on NBC, with Richard Thomas, a young actor well known for playing

John-Boy in *The Waltons,* in the role of Jim Pelosi. I was excited until the morning of the broadcast, when I read a review and learned that the role of the reporter who broke the story had been given to a man. I had in effect been written out of history. I never watched the movie.

I described in Chapter 1 being detailed to cover Representative Hugh L. Carey in his long-shot race for the Democratic gubernatorial nomination in 1974. I had loved every minute of it, but when Election Day was over, I turned back into a pumpkin, back at my desk on night rewrite. I remember where I was standing, a month or so later, when my life changed. I was working on a story and was looking up the spelling of a word in the big unabridged dictionary that resided on a stand near the middle of the newsroom. Sheldon Binn, the metropolitan desk's political editor, came up behind me. "You're going to be working for me now," he told me. "You're going to Albany."

Maybe Shelly Binn wanted me on the political staff. Maybe he had been ordered to take me. I never asked. Months earlier, a team of Columbia law students had arrived in the newsroom to interview the women on the reporting staff. The students were working under the direction of Harriet Rabb, a young law teacher who ran an employment discrimination clinic at Columbia Law School and was handling a class-action lawsuit that charged the *Times* with discriminating against its female employees in pay, assignments, and promotions. The suit had been organized by some brave older women at the paper. After attending a meeting at which Harriet Rabb gave a dazzling presentation on sex discrimination law and the *Times'* legal vulnerabilities—which were apparent simply from a glance around the newsroom—I had signed up, as had nearly all the other women, as a member of the plaintiff class. The law student who interviewed me asked what I wanted to do at the paper. No woman had ever been assigned to Albany. But I had observed the central role that time there seemed to play in the career paths of the male reporters around me. That's what I would like to do, I told the law student.

None of that was in my mind when Sheldon Binn gave me the news. My feeling was simply one of relief. He was the most beloved editor in the newsroom, and he was willing to take a chance on me. A path forward had opened. "You're going to be working for me now." In forty years at the *Times,* I never heard sweeter words.

Shelly Binn, then in his early fifties, was a World War II veteran, wounded in battle, who had come home and graduated from the University of Wisconsin. He had a glass eye and a steel plate in his head. A few years before he tapped me on the shoulder, he had survived a major heart attack. He was a classically hard-bitten newspaperman who simply loved a good story. The most prized response to be evoked from Shelly was his "No kidding!" His own politics, which he kept to himself, were to the right of most people at the *Times.* He was never going to run the paper; whether he had ever had such an ambition I don't know, but, lacking any such illusion, he was free from the sometimes poisonous distractions of office politics. He stood up for his people, judging them completely on their merits, without regard to who was in or out of favor with the higher editors. This was rare. His reward was the unflinching loyalty of the reporters who worked for him and who would do anything to keep his respect and maybe even occasionally earn his praise. In the newsroom, reporters were known to duck down the back stairs, which led to Sardi's restaurant on West

Forty-Fourth Street, when they saw certain editors approaching. In Albany, by contrast, grown men fought to be first to talk to Shelly when the bureau secretary announced that he was on the phone. The greatest pleasure of my two years as bureau chief, to which I was promoted after my first two years in Albany, was the morning phone call with Shelly to plot how we were going to handle the day's events. (Despite his wartime injuries and bad heart, Shelly Binn beat the odds, dying at eighty-three in 2006.)

The New York City fiscal crisis was a catastrophe for which no one in Albany, neither the state officials nor the journalists, was prepared by education or experience to fully grasp. The city had masked a structural budget deficit for years by borrowing ever-greater amounts at ever-higher interest rates. Finally, the credit markets lost faith in the city and shut it out, leaving it no way to refinance billions of dollars of debt. That sounds familiar today, but back then it was shocking. This is not the place to describe the details of the problem or its complex solution, except to say there was something both thrilling and frightening about climbing the learning curve along with those whose task was to find a solution. We all believed—officials and journalists alike—that we were doing the public's business.

The elected officials, members of their staffs, and the outside experts brought in from the financial world all recognized that if any solution was to work, restoring public confidence was essential. So the officials took reporters into their confidence, educating us about the basics of public finance and keeping us abreast of complicated financial moves in order to ensure that the stories would be accurate. That is not to say that there was no maneuvering among the players for political advantage, or that everyone was on the same page all the time. There were fissures between upstate and downstate, between the Republican-controlled state senate and the Democrats who ran the assembly, and between the state's legislative and executive branches. On more than a few occasions, I found myself shuttling back and forth in the corridor that connected the two houses of the legislature. My journalistic role was to get comment from the leadership of each chamber on the latest development, but inevitably I also played the secondary role of messenger, keeping each side informed of what the other was up to. But politics aside, all the players shared the same goal.

The courts were also part of this picture. In May 1975, the New York Court of Appeals was preparing to rule on the constitutionality of an important piece of the solution's architecture. The acceptance by the financial markets of the ruling would be crucial for the ultimate success of the effort. The court offered to give reporters an early look at the decision in order to give them time to digest it, and one of the judges made himself available by telephone throughout the day, on a background basis, to answer any questions a reporter might have. I availed myself of both of these unusual opportunities.[3]

Could this happen today? Could anything I have just described happen today? Part of the confidence that infused these confidential conversations came from the newsmakers' knowledge that the next deadline was at least hours away. There were no websites by which to transmit half-digested impressions of developing stories. There was time, sometimes, to pick up and start over. One night at the height of the crisis, the state senate was scheduled to take up an important bill in a late-night session that was due to begin after the newspaper's late city edition went to press. The senate's calendar was tightly controlled by its majority leader, a courtly and principled upstate Republican named Warren Anderson. So with a high degree of confidence, I filed my story for the late city paper: "The Senate tonight began debate . . ." Sitting in the press row on the senate floor, I was appalled when Senator Anderson suddenly dismissed the senate for the night without, in fact, taking up the bill. I ran up to him and explained the problem he had just created. The presses at the *New York Times* were running, printing a story that had just become untrue.

The senators were still on the floor, lingering and chatting in small groups. Without hesitation, Senator Anderson gaveled the senate back into session and directed the clerk to call up the bill. As a formal matter, that meant that debate had begun, and even though no one had actually debated anything in the remaining seconds before the majority leader sent the senators home, my story had gone in those few seconds from untrue to technically accurate.

As I think back on the fiscal crisis saga, which stretched out for much of two years, I find myself wondering what today's journalistic ethics-minders would make of some of these episodes. I didn't know any reporters who were rooting for one side or the other in a partisan sense. But it's fair to say we were rooting for a workable solution. None of us wanted to see New York City collapse into bankruptcy, shutting down services and stripping public employees of the value of their pensions. We were, most of us, New Yorkers. To that extent, our interests were aligned with the interests of the newsmakers we were covering. We were looking for heroes, not villains. We were journalists, but we were citizens, too. How would the fiscal crisis have played out in today's 24/7 media environment? I'm not sure.

Arthur Hays Sulzberger, publisher of the *Times* from 1935 to 1961, captured the newspaper's credo of impartiality with a saying: "We tell the public which way the cat is jumping. The public will take care of the cat."[4] Maybe that attitude was adequate in Sulzberger's day. Maybe it still is for sophisticated *New York Times* readers who take the trouble to sort through the cacophony of media voices retailing mutually exclusive versions of the truth. But surely we now know, in what has come to be called the post-truth age, that simply reporting which way the cat is jumping falls short if the goal of journalism is to empower readers to sort through the noise and come to their own informed conclusions.[5] For that, they need context: not just what happened a minute ago, but what led up to that minute, why it happened, and what might come next.

That sounds obvious enough, but I was well into my three decades of covering the Supreme Court before I thought consciously of this kind of reader empowerment as the goal—in fact, the highest goal—of journalism. The spur to my thinking was the Internet. When I started covering the court in 1978, there was of course no Internet, and most people didn't even have a fax machine or any other way of transmitting documents. When the court handed down a decision, copies of the opinions were immediately distributed to the waiting press corps. But there was no way of having a really informed conversation about a newly issued decision with anyone who hadn't been at the court to receive a copy. I would call a law professor or other expert and find myself having to explain over the phone what had just happened. If the supposed expert had to take my characterization at face value, what sort of expertise was I actually relying on? So I made fewer and fewer calls, and instead developed a voice of my own; people sometimes expressed surprise at how few quotes my stories contained from any source other than the opinions themselves.

Then came the Internet, followed by websites, including the court's own, that posted the full text of the decisions almost instantly. Eventually, the court also posted argument transcripts online, along with briefs and other case material. So this raised the question, what was the added value of daily journalism about the Supreme Court? It couldn't be simply to report the latest occurrence—which way the cat jumped, by a vote of five to four. Any interested reader could go to supremecourt.gov and find all the necessary information, in much greater detail, and faster.

Of course, the answer was hiding in plain sight: the added value lay in providing context. Why was this case at the Supreme Court in the first place? What legal or political forces, or both, had propelled it there? Why might the court have decided to review it? What and whose agenda did it serve? And now that it was decided, what was likely to happen next? What new legal paths were open, and which were foreclosed? What issues did the justices sweep under the rug? Which did they reach out to decide unnecessarily?

The bare documents alone—the briefs, the transcript, the opinion itself—wouldn't begin to answer those questions. But drawing on my years as a court watcher, plus my days, weeks, and months studying the cases on the ever-changing docket, I could answer them—or at least make a fair start at doing so. I had been disconcerted by the tidal wave of information the Internet brought with it. But once I found a safe place to stand—immersed but not drowning—I actually felt more enthusiastic about the job than I had in quite a while. Instead of rendering daily journalism obsolete, the Internet, it seemed to me, made my kind of reporting more useful than ever.

I never expected to cover the Supreme Court. Following the great Anthony Lewis, who established the modern Supreme Court beat after studying for a year at Harvard Law School on a Nieman Fellowship (1956–1957), the reporters who covered the court for the Times all had law degrees. I had pictured a Supreme Court assignment for a brief instant many years before. As a college student, I had applied for a coveted summer internship at the *Washington Post.* Invited to Washington for an interview, I found myself facing a panel of three editors. Among the questions they asked me was this one: If you could choose a beat to cover, would it be the

White House, Congress, the Supreme Court, or a small town in Virginia? I calculated quickly. The White House seemed too far above my station. Congress, which is what really appealed to me (in my American government major, I was placing special emphasis on the study of Congress), somehow seemed too obvious. I certainly wasn't interested in the town in Virginia. The Supreme Court, on the other hand, seemed non-obvious, enticingly intellectual: the safe choice. "The Supreme Court," I replied. Wrong! one of the editors responded. If I really wanted to learn to be a reporter, I would have picked the small town in Virginia. I suspect my body language revealed my displeasure at having been unfairly caught in a trap. I didn't get the job.

During my fourth year in Albany, I decided it was time for a career move, and I asked for a transfer to the Washington bureau. Congress seemed a logical beat. The editor I spoke with in the bureau sounded interested but noncommittal. I waited. Then I was offered an unexpected opportunity. The year before, the Ford Foundation, in cooperation with Yale Law School, had established a fellowship program for journalists. The idea was that five journalists a year would join the law school's first-year class, taking the basic courses as well as electives of their choice and receiving a master's degree at the end of the year. The goal of Fred Friendly, the Ford Foundation official who came up with the idea, was gradually to increase the law-related literacy in America's newsrooms. The *Times* had not sent anyone for the program's initial year. Would I like to join the second class?

I quickly said yes and soon found myself a student again, nine years after my college graduation. As I understood the implicit message from the editors, I was to spend the academic year in New Haven, learn some law, and then join the Washington bureau to cover the Supreme Court. Lesley Oelsner, who had covered the beat with distinction through the Watergate episode, was leaving the paper to become an assistant United States attorney in New York. Warren Weaver, a seasoned political reporter with a law degree, who had covered the court years earlier, had reluctantly agreed to fill in until the paper could find a permanent replacement. As this sequence of events suggests, the Supreme Court was not the most popular beat in Washington journalism.

Before leaving New York, I went to see Abe Rosenthal, who years earlier had treated me to his nostalgic soliloquy about his earliest years at the paper. Now he was the executive editor. I was hoping for some kind of commitment about what would happen to me after my year at Yale. "Let's see how you do in law school," was his response. (My future was not the only subject of our conversation. I asked for a raise. I had expected one when I became Albany bureau chief two years earlier, since my predecessors—all men, of course—had all received one. When no raise showed up in my first months' paychecks, I inquired about it. After a few weeks, an assistant editor on the metropolitan desk got back to me. "We've looked into it and we have decided that you're making enough," he told me. My yearly salary was then about $35,000. I recounted all this to Abe Rosenthal, who professed shock. "Why didn't you just come right to me?" he asked. The small raise that resulted was not retroactive.)

I worked hard in law school, studying to the point of exhaustion and beyond: once, having fallen into a sound sleep with my head on a desk in the library, I gradually became aware of an annoying sound. Finally opening my eyes, I saw a man with a jackhammer about ten feet from my head, prying up a tile on the floor. Naturally, after Abe Rosenthal's challenge, I wanted to be a successful law student. I had another reason as well, one of personal pride. On a bulletin board just outside the library, the staff posted each of Warren Weaver's articles from the *Times*. In the event that I actually did end up covering the court, they would post my stories, too. I didn't want people to see my byline and remember me as someone who had floundered in law school. It was not until late spring that I received official word that I was heading to Washington.

My career as the *New York Times* Supreme Court correspondent began inauspiciously. There was no *New York Times*. The printers had gone on strike in August, a strike provoked by the New York newspaper publishers to break the printers' union, and the reporters' union, the Newspaper Guild, was honoring the picket line. Many of the reporters in the Washington bureau had taken temporary jobs on Capitol Hill or in the federal agencies they covered in order to have a replacement paycheck. I decided against looking for a temporary job because I had work to do. Surely the *Times* would start publishing again, and, just as surely, I wanted to be fully prepared to start writing about the court the minute that happened.

For the next two months, I went to the court every day, sitting at the desk reserved for the *Times* in a corner of the press room and reading through the new petitions from which the court would build its docket for the 1978 term that was about to begin. This turned out to be the best possible use of my time. I wasn't breaking the strike; I was serving myself, not the paper. By good fortune, a new publication, the *National Law Journal,* had just started up, and it paid me well for occasional stories from the court. More important, this fallow period showed me how little I knew about the Supreme Court and its procedures, and gave me time to get acclimated. For example, I had no idea that the justices reviewed new petitions not just once at the start of the term but continually; just when I had at first thought my work was done, a new list of cases landed on my desk. The experience showed me how little law students actually learn about the court beneath the level of high theory. Decades later, when I began teaching at Yale Law School, I channeled that experience, along with my own subsequent learning, into a course I called The Institutional Supreme Court. I offered it as a spring-semester elective to first-year students, whose curiosity about the court had been piqued by their fall-term courses. The course always had a waiting list.

I was welcomed by the dozen or so other regulars in the press room, who were generous in explaining the court's mysteries. A few of my new colleagues had law degrees. Most just had wisdom gained through experience, and many became good friends. (Yes, we were also professional competitors, but it was not really a competitive beat, since it didn't rely on sources and everyone received the same information at the same time.) On busy argument or decision days, several dozen reporters would show up at the court. But only a relative handful came day in and day out, even when the court wasn't sitting, to study the incoming cases and prepare for the next round of announcements on which new cases the justices had accepted for full briefing and argument. Either a grant or a denial might make news. Advance preparation was essential because the weekly "order list" consisted simply of a list of cases by name and docket number. With fifty or more cases on each list, the Monday morning distribution was not the time to start figuring out whether anything noteworthy had occurred. There was only one copy of each petition on the press room shelves, and no machine with which to copy a petition. (There was a single, antique copying machine that could be fed one sheet at a time, but the petitions came as bound booklets.) The only way to prepare was by taking notes, just like an old-fashioned student. It was a good habit, one I maintained over the years, long after a modern copying machine arrived in the press room and after many petitions appeared online. These developments made it much easier to report on deadline about the grant of a new case, and eventually very few reporters bothered to look at the petitions in advance. But I continued to find it an invaluable way to keep track of the raw material from which the Supreme Court constructs its docket and, in doing so, sets the country's legal agenda. Besides, I had a recurring nightmare that the court had granted a case that had escaped my notice and about which I could offer my editors no information.

By the time the printers' strike ended in November 1978, I was still climbing a steep learning curve, but I was ready to go to work. My years in Albany had shown me how much fun covering politics could be, and I understood why members of the Washington press corps were not clamoring to cover the Supreme Court. Contact with the justices ranged from zero to minimal.

The work consisted not of the back-corridor schmoozing that marked life in Albany but rather of sitting and reading. It also quickly occurred to me that while political reporting has a rather generous margin of error—what might be wrong today could well be right tomorrow—it was frighteningly easy to be simply wrong about a Supreme Court decision. I was never flatly wrong, but I missed plenty in those early years, through a failure to appreciate the significance of developments in doctrinal areas with which I was unfamiliar.

I arrived midway through the life of the Burger court (1969–1986). Chief Justice Warren E. Burger was press averse to the point of paranoia. *The Brethren,* an insiders' tell-all book by Bob Woodward and Scott Armstrong, had just been published. The book cast Chief Justice Burger in a highly unflattering light and exposed the disdain that some members of the court had for him, particularly Justice Potter Stewart, a major source for the authors. The atmosphere inside the court was charged with a fear of leaks. The justices' law clerks were told that they would be fired if seen talking to a reporter. A question commonly asked of Supreme Court reporters in those days was whether they would publish a leak if they ever obtained one. Implicit in the question was a challenge: Would you be loyal to journalism, or to the court? That seemed to me a false choice. I always replied that if I were absolutely confident that the leaked material was authentic, of course I would write the story. I didn't feel an abstract loyalty to the court. What I owed it, it seemed to me, was attention and accuracy. I never got a leak of any kind from the court. Occasionally, people inside and outside the court assumed I had. But what looked like inside information—for instance, a story reporting that a justice, having failed to hold a majority, had been forced to surrender an opinion to a justice who had previously voted in dissent—was the result of speculation informed by close observation of voting patterns and the monthly distribution of opinion assignments. You could learn a lot just by paying attention.

In June 1981, just months into President Ronald Reagan's first term, Potter Stewart announced his retirement. Reagan had made a campaign pledge to appoint the first woman to the court. He chose Sandra Day O'Connor, an obscure judge then sitting on Arizona's intermediate-level court. I had never heard her name. She fascinated me. Only a few years earlier, the notion of a woman on the Supreme Court had been played for laughs in a popular Broadway play, *First Monday in October*. I covered her Senate confirmation hearing, presided over with almost parodic Southern politeness by Senator Strom Thurmond. It was the first time I had covered anything in Congress since coming to Washington, and I enjoyed it. It was also the first televised Supreme Court confirmation hearing, and the senators played to the camera. So did the nominee, but, unlike the senators, she was subtle: charming, on message, a little remote, an obvious winner.

I felt a jolt of excitement when I first saw Justice O'Connor on the bench. I wouldn't have predicted such a powerful reaction to seeing a woman seated there. She entered my dream life. Years later, when a crucial abortion case was pending and there was every reason to think that Justice O'Connor would join others in voting to disavow *Roe v. Wade* and overturn the constitutional right to abortion, I had a vivid dream that I was seated with the justices at their conference table. In the dream, Justice O'Connor turned to me and said, "Linda, what do you think we should do?"

Abortion became an important theme of my coverage of the court. The court had decided a few abortion cases during my first years on the beat, but because nothing seemed to shake the court's support for the right to abortion, the news value of these few decisions was limited. That changed on June 15, 1983, when the court announced its decision in what had appeared to be a routine abortion case from Akron, Ohio.[6] The city had imposed an array of restrictions on access to abortion, including a twenty-four-hour waiting period, a second-trimester hospitalization requirement, and a requirement for doctors to seek a patient's informed consent by following a script intended to dissuade the woman from terminating her pregnancy. A federal district court had invalidated most of the restrictions, relying on *Roe v. Wade* and the Supreme Court's subsequent rulings. The Supreme Court followed suit in an opinion by Justice Lewis F. Powell Jr., who summarized the decision from the bench. The vote was six to three to strike down the Akron ordinance. Justice Powell announced that the author of the dissenting opinion was Justice Sandra Day O'Connor.

Sitting in the press section of the courtroom, I was in a state of shock. How could the first female Supreme Court justice, whose arrival had touched me so deeply, betray women in this way? Her dissenting opinion, when I read it a few minutes later, was even worse than I had imagined, a broadside attack on "the Roe framework," which, she declared, "is clearly on a collision course with itself." While antiabortion activism had clearly played a role in Ronald Reagan's election, the issue had remained largely abstract to me, on the assumption that no matter what happened in politics, the Supreme Court remained committed to its precedent and to protecting the basic right. In fact, the only objection to Sandra O'Connor's nomination two years earlier had come from right-to-life forces in Arizona and on Capitol Hill, fretful that her thoroughly opaque record on abortion disqualified her from appointment by a president whose party platform called for the appointment of judges who would overturn *Roe v. Wade*. But now it appeared that those concerns were not well founded, and that the court's adherence to the status quo was in doubt.

Abortion presented a challenge to me, clearly, in that I knew my own position and I knew how I wanted the court to rule. But in this regard, it wasn't qualitatively different from other subjects I wrote about. For example, I wanted the court to preserve the right to habeas corpus, under constant attack from my earliest years on the beat. I wanted the court to maintain its vigilance in insisting on desegregation remedies in the public schools, a position the Burger court was backing away from at a rapid pace. Much later, I wanted the court to disallow the legal black hole the George W. Bush administration had established at Guantánamo Bay.

Anyone who knew me would have known my positions on these issues and others. My colleagues at the *Times* did, long before the public abortion-related controversies. Every year, the publisher solicited employees to authorize a payroll deduction for contributions to United Way. When I worked in New York, I always contributed after checking the list of United Way beneficiaries and seeing that Planned Parenthood was on the list. When I arrived in Washington, I checked the list and was surprised to find that the local Planned Parenthood affiliate was missing. I called United Way in Washington to ask why. After being passed among several employees, I finally reached someone who told me that the problem was that Planned Parenthood was "controversial." I replied that I didn't see much controversy in curbing the high teen pregnancy rate in the District of Columbia, and that I would henceforth make my own contribution directly to Planned Parenthood. I described this encounter in a letter to Arthur O. Sulzberger, the *Times* publisher, and posted a copy of my letter on the office bulletin board, urging colleagues to follow my example. If anyone did, they kept that knowledge to themselves.

I continued to send a check to Planned Parenthood every month for the rest of my career. I turned down the option, which charities much prefer, of an automatic monthly deduction from my checking account. It was important to me to write a check every month and sign my name. It was the signature of a citizen. The stories that appeared under my byline, on abortion and all other subjects, were the work of a journalist. If anyone ever thought those failed to measure up to professional standards, they never told me or anyone else.

I retired from the *Times* in July 2008, almost forty years to the day after I started my internship with James Reston. The time was right. My editors had shielded me from the task of filing for the website within minutes after an opinion was issued. I kept to my old deadlines: a summary of the story or stories by three o'clock, final copy by six. That couldn't have lasted much longer.

None of my press room colleagues was excused from feeding the beast. I could have done it, too—remember, the *Crimson* had trained me to be fast—and I would have taken a certain satisfaction, I'm sure, in being both fast and right. But I'm not sure I could have been fast and deep—or at least, not as deep as I liked to think I could be with hours, rather than minutes, at my disposal.

As a result of the pressure of the web on my colleagues, I often felt lonely in the press room. I had cherished my relationships there. For years, we had shared lunches as we dissected cases and talked about the court in a private language that few back in our respective offices would understand or care about. Now, no one had time for collegiality. The press room was usually empty by lunchtime, and I often ate alone. I had begun to feel confined by the daily beat. In 2004, with the paper's full support and a three-month summer leave of absence, I wrote a biography of Justice Harry A. Blackmun, based on his newly opened trove of personal and official papers at the Library of Congress. The book, *Becoming Justice Blackmun,* was published in 2005 and was a critical and commercial success. With our daughter off in college, I felt free to accept more speaking invitations and travel more extensively. I published several law review articles. It thrilled me to be in direct conversation with a new kind of audience.

An incident at the end of the 2006–2007 term had alarmed me. The Roberts court, in its second term and now fully operational with Justice Samuel A. Alito Jr. having replaced Justice O'Connor the previous January, had taken a sharp turn to the right, most notably in a decision upholding the federal Partial-Birth Abortion Ban Act and another rejecting voluntary integration plans in Louisville and Seattle.[7] Both were decided by votes of five to four; had Justice O'Connor still been on the court, the decisions would have been five to four the other way.

For my end-of-term wrap-up story, I began, "It was the Supreme Court that conservatives had long yearned for and that liberals feared. By the time the Roberts court ended its first full term on Thursday, the picture was clear. This was a conservative court." I filed the story and, still at my desk some time later, was approached by a rather sheepish Washington bureau chief. The executive editor had an objection, he told me. I couldn't say on my own authority, without the cover of a news analysis label, that it was a "conservative court."

At first, I didn't think I had heard correctly. Then, as it sank in, I decided that I could play this game, too. Fine, I said, if the executive editor wants to change it, he can take my byline off the story. Withholding a byline is a rare, and ultimate, statement of protest by a journalist. Clearly, as I knew, that wouldn't fly for the lead of the Sunday paper.

How about just calling it a news analysis, my increasingly desperate boss asked. No, I said, I'm simply stating a fact. It *is* a conservative court.

He went back to his office for further consultation with New York. He came back to my desk. Suppose we said it was a "more conservative court." More than what? I asked. More than it was before, he answered.

This seemed silly, but, at the same time, a needless place to draw a line in the sand. Clearly, the bureau chief had worked out a face-saving compromise for the executive editor. Sure, I said, it's a more conservative court.

So now the story that ran on July 1, 2007—with my byline and without a "news analysis" label—began,

It was the Supreme Court that conservatives had long yearned for and that liberals feared.

By the time the Roberts court ended its first full term on Thursday, the picture was clear. This was a more conservative court, sometimes muscularly so, sometimes more tentatively, its majority sometimes differing on methodology but agreeing on the outcome in cases big and small.[8]

I didn't know it at the time, but I would write only one more end-of-term story. In February 2008, the paper offered a newsroom-wide buyout. Given my forty years' tenure, the terms were generous. I put my hand up. I would leave after the term ended. I had no definite plan in mind. Maybe—after two dozen trips to Mexico—I would finally manage to learn Spanish and work with the growing immigrant community in Montgomery County, Maryland, where we lived. Word of my decision spread in legal circles. By the time a week was out, my husband and I had accepted an offer from Harold Hongju Koh, dean of Yale Law School, to come and teach, beginning the following spring.

Shortly after I left the paper, a solicitation arrived from the Montgomery County board of elections, seeking volunteers to serve as Election Day judges for the upcoming presidential election. I suppose I had received these before but had tossed them automatically, since service of that kind was out of the question for a working journalist—even aside from the fact that the Supreme Court was always in session on Election Day. I signed up. You had to identify as either a Democratic judge or a Republican judge. I was a Democrat. I took my two days of training: how to help voters unfamiliar with the voting machine, what to do when various problems or confusions arose. For Election Day, I was assigned to a polling place in a neighborhood near the National Institutes of Health. There were a number of new citizens, first-time voters. I arrived as scheduled before dawn and stayed with my fellow election judges until nearly midnight, after we had secured the voting machines and tallied the results for transmission to the central office at the county seat in Rockville. Barack Obama was certainly the winner in Montgomery County, but that was no surprise. I had no idea what was happening in the rest of the country.

I got in my car and turned on the radio. It was raining and, as I feared, I got lost on the unfamiliar roads. Obama seemed to have carried Virginia. That had to be a good sign. I had been on my feet for eighteen hours but I wasn't tired. As I navigated winding suburban roads looking for a recognizable intersection, I felt a wave of exhilaration from more than the election outcome. The day and night had been intensely interesting. I had learned things that might well have been useful journalistically, such as what happens when a would-be voter is sent to the judges' table and instructed to cast a provisional ballot. But I no longer had to justify, even to myself, my participation in the mechanics of citizenship. I hadn't been there to learn. I had been there to engage fully, if briefly, in the core process of democracy. I had spent the day and night as a citizen, just a citizen. It felt exactly right. I kept driving. Soon enough, I found my bearings, and then I was home.

Notes

Index

NOTES

1. BOUNDARIES

1. Seymour P. Lachman, *The Man Who Saved New York: Hugh Carey and the Great Fiscal Crisis of 1975* (Albany, NY: State University of New York Press, 2010).

2. For example, see Melissa Lafsky, "The Greenhouse Effect: Can Reporters and Opinions Ever Really Mix?," *Huffington Post,* September 27, 2006, http://www.huffingtonpost.com/eat-the-press/2006/09/27/the-greenhouse-effect-ca_e_30372.html.

3. Michael Barbaro, "Trump Gives Up a Lie but Refuses to Repent," *New York Times,* September 17, 2016, A1.

4. Peter Beinart, "The Death of 'He Said, She Said' Journalism," *Atlantic,* September 19, 2016, http://www.theatlantic.com/politics/archive/2016/09/the-death-of-he-said-she-said-journalism.

5. Radcliffe College is now the Radcliffe Institute of Advanced Study.

6. Rasul v. Bush, 542 U.S. 466 (2004).

7. Planned Parenthood v. Casey, 505 U.S. 833 (1992).

8. Lawrence v. Texas, 539 U.S. 558 (2003).

9. David Folkenflik, "Critics Question Reporter's Airing of Personal Views," September 26, 2006, http://www.npr.org/templates/story/story.php?storyId=6146693 (accessed April 15, 2017).

10. The September 28, 2006, interview appeared only on the web. An archived copy can be found at archive.li/Vfnc9.

11. Douglas Johnson, legislative director of the National Right to Life Committee, when asked by the *Columbia Journalism Review* about an earlier controversy over my participation in a march in favor of abortion rights (to which I refer later in this chapter), said that although he had assumed that I was in favor of the right to abortion, "of people who regularly cover abortion issues, whose stories are consistently unbalanced, she would not be on the short list." Stephanie Saul, "Judgment Call: Do Reporters Have a Right to March?," *Columbia Journalism Review,* July / August 1989, 50.

12. Byron Calame, "Spotting Freelancer Conflicts: A Solution with Problems," *New York Times,* January 28, 2007, http://www.nytimes.com/2007/01/28/opinion/ 28pubed.html.

13. This letter one of six that appeared in the public editor's column of February 4, 2007 under the headline: "Other Voices: Conflicts, Opinions, and More Disclosures; What Reporters Think."

14. Paul McLeary, "Michael Gordon's Molehill Becomes a Mountain," *Columbia Journalism Review,* January 2007, http://www.cjr.org/behind_the_news /michael_gordons_molehill_becom.php.

15. Eleanor Randolph, "The Media and the March: The Ethics of Joining the Abortion Protest," *Washington Post,* April 15, 1989, C4.

16. Quoted in Mitchell Stephens, *Beyond News: The Future of Journalism* (New York: Columbia University Press, 2014), 119.

17. Randolph, "Media and the March," C4.

18. Carlo Pizzati, "La Marcia Proibita di Linda," *Prima International,* June 1989, 85.

19. Max Frankel, *The Times of My Life and My Life with "The Times"* (New York: Random House, 1999), 517.

20. See, for example, Gene Foreman, *The Ethical Journalist* (Malden, MA: Wiley-Blackwell, 2010), 144–145.

21. Michael S. Rosenwald, "NPR Host Diane Rehm Emerges as Key Force in the Right-to-Die Debate," *Washington Post,* February 14, 2015.

22. Elizabeth Jensen, "Diane Rehm, Personal Politics and the Ethical Reach of NPR," *NPR,* February 25, 2015, http://www.npr.org/sections /ombudsman/2015/02/25/388723154/diane-rehm -personal-politics-and-the-ethical-reach-of-npr.

23. Benjamin Mullin, "NPR Updates Ethics Policy after Ombud Raises Political Advocacy Questions," *Poynter MediaWire,* March 26, 2015, http://www.poynter.org/news/mediawire/330119 /npr-updates-ethics-policy-following-advocacy -questions/.

24. Elizabeth Jensen, "Rehm to Step Away from Fundraising Role," *NPR,* March 9, 2015, http://www.npr.org/sections/ombudsman/2015/03/09 /391230157/rehm-to-step-away-from-fundraising -role.

2. HABITS

1. David Barstow, "'Up Is Down': Trump's Unreality Show Echoes His Business Past," *New York Times,* January 28, 2017, A1.

2. Michael Barbaro, "Trump Gives Up a Lie but Refuses to Repent," *New York Times,* September 17, 2016, A1.

3. Michael D. Shear and Emmarie Huetteman, "Meeting with Top Lawmakers, Trump Repeats

an Election Lie," *New York Times,* January 24, 2017, A1.

4. Lauren Carroll, "At CNN Debate, Carly Fiorina Urges Others to Watch Planned Parenthood Videos," www.politifact.com/truth-o-meter /statements/2015/sep/17/carly-fiorina/cnndebate -carly-fiorina-urges-others-watch-planne /(September 17, 2015).

5. Margaret Sullivan, "Wanted: A Tougher Approach to Truth," *New York Times,* October 4, 2015, SR10.

6. Michael Scherer, "Questions Remain over whether Video Carly Fiorina Cited in Debate Shows Abortion," *Time,* September 29, 2015, http://www.time .com/4055143/abortion-carly-fiorina-planned -parenthood/.

7. Bill Barrow, "Fiorina Not Backing Down on Distortion of Planned Parenthood, Uses It as Campaign Centerpiece," *U.S. News and World Report,* October 3, 2015, http://www.usnews.com/news/politics/articles /2015/10/03/fiorina-makes-distortion-of-planned -parenthood-a-centerpiece.

8. Jake Tapper, "Checking Carly Fiorina's Claims about an Anti-abortion Video," *CNN,* October 5, 2015, http://www.cnn.com/2015/10/05/politics/fact -check-carly-fiorina-anti-abortion-videos.

9. Dave Levitan, "Doubling Down on Falsehoods," FactCheck.org, September 22, 2015, http://www .factcheck.org/2015/09/doubling-down-on -falsehoods/.

10. Linda Greenhouse, "Challenging 'He Said, She Said' Journalism," *Nieman Reports,* July 6, 2012, http://www.niemanreports.org/articles/challenging-he -said-she-said-journalism/.

11. Eric Lipton and Ashley Parker, "Immigration Poses Threat of Another Republican Rift," *New York Times,* October 25, 2013.

12. Mitchell Stephens, *Beyond News: The Future of Journalism* (New York: Columbia University Press, 2014), 102.

13. Ibid., 129.

14. Ibid., xxvi.

15. Bill Kovach and Tom Rosenstiel, *The Elements of Journalism: What Newspeople Should Know and the Public Should Expect,* 3rd ed. (New York: Three Rivers, 2014), 97–136.

16. Ibid., 103.

17. Margaret Sullivan, "Another Outbreak of 'False Balance'?," *New York Times,* February 8, 2015.

18. Aaron Blake, "GOP Congressman Calls Obama a Socialist Dictator," *Washington Post,* January 28, 2014; Robert G. Kaiser, "How Republicans Lost Their Mind, Democrats Lost Their Souls and Washington Lost Its Appeal," *Washington Post,* February 28, 2014.

19. John Koblin, "A Sarcastic Critic of Politics and Media, Signing Off," *New York Times,* August 6, 2015, B1.

20. Jay Rosen, "NPR News Analyst: How Juan Williams Got Fired," *PressThink,* October 24, 2010, http://pressthink.org/2010/10/npr-news-analyst-how-juan-williams-got-fired. In Rosen's description, "the view from nowhere is a professional ideology that positions the news provider between polarized extremes. It tries to generate trust by advertising the agendalessness of the journalist."

21. Michael Wines, "Fraud at the Polls Was Miniscule, Despite Claims," *New York Times,* December 19, 2016, A1.

22. Veasey v. Abbott, 830 F. 3d 216, 238-9 (5th Cir. 2016).

23. North Carolina State Conference of NAACP v. McCrory, 831 F.3d 204 (4th Cir. 2016).

24. Trip Gabriel, "He Pushed Kansas to the Right. Now Kansas Is Pushing Back," *New York Times,* October 17, 2014, A1.

25. Timothy Williams, "Federal Judge Orders Ohio to Undo Cuts to Early Voting," *New York Times,* September 5, 2014, A14.

26. Margaret Sullivan, "So We Beat On: Another Year in the Hot Seat," *New York Times,* October 19, 2014, SR12.

27. Julie Bosman, "Voter ID Battle Shifts to Kansas," *New York Times,* October 16, 2015, A1.

28. David T. Z. Mindich, *Just the Facts: How "Objectivity" Came to Define American Journalism* (New York: New York University Press, 1998), 7.

29. Thomas E. Patterson, *Informing the News* (New York: Vintage Books, 2013), 40–41.

30. See Linda Greenhouse, "Abortion at the Supreme Court's Door," *New York Times,* October 15, 2015, http://www.nytimes.com/2015/10/15/opinion/abortion-at-the-supreme-courts-door.html. The eventual decision was *Whole Woman's Health v. Hellerstedt,* 136 S. Ct. 2292 (2016).

31. Adam Liptak, "Supreme Court Takes Abortion Case from Texas," *New York Times,* November 14, 2015, A1. Oddly, an earlier article, reporting the Supreme Court's granting of a temporary stay that allowed the clinics to remain open, used nearly the same formulation with one exception: instead of "intended to put many of them out of business," the earlier story was a shade more pointed: "a ruse meant to put many of them out of business." Adam Liptak

and Manny Fernandez, "Supreme Court Allows Texas Abortion Clinics to Remain Open," *New York Times,* June 29, 2015, A12.

32. Sandhya Somashekhar, "Abortion Foes' Strategy Faces a Key Test at the Supreme Court," *Washington Post,* February 22, 2016.

33. Guttmacher Institute, *Induced Abortion in the United States* (New York: Guttmacher Institute, January 2017), http://www.guttmacher.org/fact-sheet/induced -abortion-united-states.

34. See Linda Greenhouse and Reva B. Siegel, "Casey and the Clinic Closings: When 'Protecting Health' Obstructs Choice," *Yale Law Journal* 125, no. 5 (March 2016): 1428, 1444–1449.

35. Michael Schudson, *The Rise of the Right to Know: Politics and the Culture of Transparency, 1945–1975* (Cambridge, MA: Belknap Press of Harvard University Press, 2015), 177.

36. Brent Cunningham, "Re-Thinking Objectivity," *Columbia Journalism Review,* July / August 2003, 26.

37. Stephens, *Beyond News,* 115.

38. See http://www.cjlf.org/about/history.htm (accessed May 16, 2017).

39. Criminal Justice Legal Foundation 2015 IRS Form 990 filing, available from ProPublica, https:// projects.propublica.org/nonprofits/organizations /942798865.

40. Rick Lyman, "Ohio Execution Using Untested Drug Cocktail Renews the Debate over Lethal Injections," *New York Times,* January 17, 2014, A15.

41. Erik Eckholm, "Juveniles Facing Lifelong Terms Despite Rulings," *New York Times,* January 20, 2014, A1.

42. Jesse McKinley, "After Defeat by Filibuster, a California Justice Pick," *New York Times,* July 27, 2011, A12.

43. Adam Liptak, "Number of Inmates on Death Row Declines as Challenges to Justice System Rise," *New York Times,* January 11, 2003.

44. Richard Wolf, "Does the Death Penalty Serve a Purpose? Supreme Court Hasn't Decided Either," *USA Today,* December 12, 2016.

45. Felicity Barringer, "Appeals Panel Cuts Award in Valdez Spill by Exxon," *New York Times,* December 23, 2006.

46. Michael S. Schmidt, "Vick Begins Serving Time ahead of Sentencing," *New York Times,* November 20, 2007.

47. Sabrina Tavernise, "Charges Filed in Peanut Salmonella Case," *New York Times,* February 21, 2013.

48. Danielle Ivory, "VW Hires Feinberg to Create Compensation Plan," *New York Times,* December 18, 2015, B1.

49. Steve Eder, "Trump University Lawsuits May Not Be Closed After All," *New York Times,* March 6, 2017, A12.

50. Adam Liptak and Eric Lichtblau, "Judge Finds Wiretap Actions Violate the Law," *New York Times,* August 18, 2006, A1.

51. Charlie Savage, "Judge Rules Some Prisoners at Bagram Have Right to Habeas Corpus," *New York Times,* April 3, 2009, A1.

52. Scott Shane and Mark Mazzetti, "Records Show Strict Rules for C.I.A. Interrogations," *New York Times,* August 26, 2009, A1.

53. R. Jeffrey Smith, "Justice Dept. Memos' Careful Legalese Obscured Harsh Reality," *Washington Post,* April 19, 2009, A4.

54. Adam Liptak, "The Power of Authority: A Dark Tale," *New York Times,* December 30, 2007.

55. Peter Baker, "Assessing the Balance of Power in an Era of Widespread Mistrust," *New York Times,* February 26, 2015, A16. Rivkin was identified in the story as "a lawyer who served in the administrations of Ronald Reagan and the first George Bush and who has worked on constitutional challenges to Mr. Obama's actions." (He devised one of the early challenges to the Affordable Care Act.)

56. Kovach and Rosenstiel, *Elements of Journalism,* 9.

57. Ibid., 9–10.

58. Martin Arnold, "The Greatest Times Editorial, Ever?," *Traditions of the Times* (unpublished newsletter, July 6, 2009).

59. Mindich, *Just the Facts,* 116 (citing Charles G. Ross, *The Writing of News: A Handbook with Chapters on Newspaper Correspondence and Copy Reading* [New York: Henry Holt and Company, 1911]). Mindich notes that "Ross's book may be the first to contain a reference to journalistic 'objectivity.'"

60. Ibid., 116.

61. Michael Schudson, "The Objectivity Norm in American Journalism," *Journalism* 2 (August 2001): 149, 162–163.

62. Ibid., 149.

63. Ibid., 162.

64. David S. Broder, *Behind the Front Page: A Candid Look at How the News Is Made* (New York: Simon and Schuster, 1987), 137–139.

65. Neal Desai et al., "Torture at Times: Water-boarding in the Media," Joan Shorenstein Center on the Press, Politics and Public Policy, April 2010, https://dash.harvard.edu/handle/1/4420886.

66. Brian Stelter, "Study of Waterboarding Coverage Prompts a Debate in the Press," *New York Times,* July 2, 2010.

67. Ibid.

68. Arthur S. Brisbane, "The Other Torture Debate," *New York Times,* May 15, 2011, WK8.

69. Dean Baquet, "The Executive Editor on the Word 'Torture,'" August 7, 2014, http://www.nytimes.com/times-insider/2014/08/07/the-executive-editor-on-the-word-torture/?_r=0.

70. Barbaro, "Trump Gives Up a Lie," A1.

71. "Times Editor Dean Baquet on Calling Out Donald Trump's Lies," by Susan Lehman, *New York Times,* podcast, September 23, 2016, http://www.nytimes.com/2016/09/23/insider/times-editor-dean-baquet-on-calling-out-donald-trumps-lies.html.

72. Quoted in Mitchell Stephens, *Beyond News: The Future of Journalism* (New York: Columbia University Press, 2014), 119.

73. Alexander Meiklejohn, *Political Freedom: The Constitutional Powers of the People* (New York: Oxford University Press, 1965), 75.

74. Calvin Trillin, *Jackson, 1964: And Other Dispatches from Fifty Years of Reporting on Race in America* (New York: Random House, 2016), xv–xvi.

75. Ibid., xvi.

76. Ibid., xvii–xviii.

77. Mike James, comment on Linda Greenhouse, "Scalia's Putsch at the Supreme Court," *New York Times,* January 21, 2016, https://www.nytimes.com/2016/01/21/opinion/scalias-putsch-at-the-supreme-court.html.

78. "RJF," comment on Linda Greenhouse, "The Broken Supreme Court," *New York Times,* April 13, 2017, https://www.nytimes.com/2017/04/13/opinion/the-broken-supreme-court.html.

79. John Gapper, "New York Times Editor Accuses Cable Networks of Blurring Lines," *Financial Times,* October 28, 2016.

80. Julie Hirschfeld Davis and David E. Sanger, "Trump Falsely Says U.S. Claim of Russian Hacking Came after Election," *New York Times,* December 15, 2016.

81. Trip Gabriel and Alan Rappeport, "Cruz Aides Spread False Rumors in Iowa that Carson Was Quitting," *New York Times,* February 6, 2016, A13.

82. Maggie Haberman, "Trump Deflects Withering Fire on Muslim Plan," *New York Times,* December 9, 2015, A1.

83. Margaret Sullivan, "A New Emphasis on Fact-Checking in Real Time," *New York Times,* December 15, 2015, http://publiceditor.blogs.nytimes.com/2015/12/15 /a-new-emphasis-on-fact-checking-in-real-time/?rref =collection%2Fcolumn%2Fthe-public-editor&action =click&contentCollection=opinion&region=stream& module=stream_unit&version=search&contentPlacement =1&pgtype=collection.

84. Ashley Parker and Jonathan Martin, "Trump Takes a Female, Hispanic Governor to Task," *New York Times,* May 26, 2016, A17.

85. Patrick Healy and Jonathan Martin, "Republican Party Unravels over Donald Trump's Takeover," *New York Times,* May 8, 2016, A1.

86. Patrick Healy and Alexander Burns, "Trump's Goal: Stay on Script about Clinton," *New York Times,* August 25, 2016, A1.

87. Patrick Healy and Thomas Kaplan, "Old Political Tactic Is Revived: Exploiting Fear, Not Easing It," *New York Times,* June 15, 2016, A1.

88. The article by Josh Lederman of the Associated Press ran, for example, in the *Berkshire Eagle* on August 12,

2016, under the headline "Trump Sticks with False Claim Obama Founded Islamic State."

89. Jim Rutenberg, "The Challenge Trump Poses to Objectivity," *New York Times,* August 8, 2016, A1.

90. James Poniewozik, "In Battle of Candidates, Lauer Is the Loser," *New York Times,* September 9, 2016, A14.

91. Ethan Coen, "2016 Thank You Notes," *New York Times,* November 11, 2016, SR2.

92. Maggie Haberman and Alexander Burns, "A Week of Whoppers from Trump," *New York Times,* September 25, 2016, A25.

93. Max Fisher and Kitty Bennett, "Our Articles on the Attacks Trump Says the Media Didn't Cover," *New York Times,* February 7, 2017, https://www.nytimes .com/2017/02/07/us/politics/the-white-house-list-of -terror-attacks-underreported-by-media.html?emc =eta1&_r=0.

94. "Covering Trump the Reuters Way," Reuters PR blog post, January 31, 2017, http://www.reuters .com/article/rpb-adlertrump-idUSKBN15F276.

95. Elizabeth Jensen, "The Pros and Cons of NPR's Policy of Not Calling Out 'Lies,'" *NPR,* January 26, 2017, http://www.npr.org/sections/ombudsman/2017 /01/26/511798707/the-pros-and-cons-of-nprs-policy -of-not-calling-out-lies.

96. "'*New York Times*' Executive Editor on the New Terrain of Covering Trump," interview with Dean Baquet by Terry Gross, *Fresh Air,* NPR, December 8, 2016, http://www.npr.org/2016/12/08 /504806512/new-york-times-executive-editor-on-the -new-terrain-of-covering-trump. A month after the inauguration, the *Times* unveiled a new branding strategy built around "Truth." The slogans included,

"Truth. It's what we search for every day" (which appeared as a full-page house ad on February 24, 2017) and "Truth. It's more important now than ever." This last appeared as a glossy poster-size insert in the newspaper on February 25. The poster included sixteen sentences beginning with the words "The truth," of which the penultimate sentence read, "The truth requires taking a stand." A *Times* commercial built around the campaign ran during the nationally televised Academy Awards on February 26. At the same time, the *Washington Post* unveiled its own new slogan: "Democracy dies in darkness."

3. CHANGES

1. Charles B. Lenahan, "Connecticut's Silent Press," *Hamden Chronicle*, April 1967.

2. Sam Roberts, "Arthur Gelb, Critic and Editor Who Shaped the Times, Dies at 90," *New York Times,* May 20, 2014, A1.

3. I described this episode in Linda Greenhouse, "Telling the Court's Story: Justice and Journalism at the Supreme Court," *Yale Law Journal* 105 (1996): 1537, 1544.

4. Quoted in Martin Arnold, "The Greatest Times Editorial, Ever?," *Traditions of the Times* (unpublished newsletter, July 2009).

5. Susan B. Glasser, "Covering Politics in a 'Post-truth' America," Brookings Institution, December 2, 2016, https://www.brookings.edu/essay/covering -politics-in-a-post-truth-america/.

6. Akron v. Akron Center for Reproductive Health, 462 U.S. 416 (1983).

7. Gonzales v. Carhart, 550 U.S. 124 (2007); Parents Involved in Community Schools v. Seattle School District No. 1, 551 U.S. 701 (2007).

8. Linda Greenhouse, "In Steps Big and Small, Supreme Court Moved Right," *New York Times,* July 1, 2007, A1.

INDEX

Index

Index